Series Consultant: Harry Smith
Author: Viv Halksworth

Audio for Speaking and Listening at your fingertips

Scan the audio QR codes to immediately launch high-quality recordings of native speakers. These are exam-style tracks for realistic assessment practice and can particularly help you with:

- **Listening: Dictation task practice**
  Listen in full, then in parts, then in full, for exam-style practice.
- **Speaking: Reading aloud practice**
  Targeted pronunciation practice of sounds helps build your confidence.
- **Speaking: Role play practice**
  Hear the teacher part and speak your answers in the pauses.

Support for longer writing tasks

Space is provided in this Workbook but sometimes you'll need to use your own paper too. Full sample student responses are given in the answer section so that you can self-assess. Remember that there is more than one correct answer for this type of question.

Practice papers

Help to check that you are exam-ready with a full set of practice papers containing exam-style questions for Listening, Speaking, Reading and Writing, for both Foundation and Higher tier.

Higher and Foundation tiers

Content that only applies to Higher Tier is marked with an

Difficulty scale

The icon next to each exam-style question tells you how difficult it is.

Some questions cover a range of difficulties.

Also available:

The Revision Guide helps you revise vocabulary and grammar with a manageable topic-by-topic approach. Worked example questions and pages on each exam paper will build your skills ready for assessment, and digital resources such as quick quizzes, vocab checks, videos and flashcards are all included!

AQA publishes the only official Sample Assessment Material on its website. The questions in this Workbook have been designed to familiarise you with the type of tasks you may meet in the exam, and are tailored to help you to practise specific skills. Remember that the actual assessments may not look like this.

Contents

Identity and relationships with others
1. Introducing yourself
2. Physical descriptions
3. Character descriptions
4. Family
5. What makes a good friend
6. Relationships
7. Helping a friend

Healthy living and lifestyle
8. Food and drink
9. Healthy eating
10. Sport and exercise
11. Physical wellbeing
12. Mental wellbeing
13. Role models in sport
14. Sporting events

Education and work
15. School subjects
16. School subjects – likes and dislikes
17. The school day
18. School facilities
19. School uniform
20. Activities in class
21. School rules
22. The good and the bad about school
23. School clubs and activities
24. How to be a good student
25. Options at 16
26. Future study plans
27. Future plans
28. Part-time jobs and money
29. Opinions about jobs
30. The pros and cons of different jobs
31. Job adverts
32. Applying for jobs
33. Preparing for interviews
34. Working to help others

Free-time activities
35. Free-time activities
36. Music and dance
37. Music and dance events
38. Reading
39. Television
40. The cinema
41. What's the story?

Customs, festivals and celebrations
42. Everyday life
43. Meals at home
44. Celebrations
45. Customs and festivals
46. Spanish festivals
47. Latin American festivals

Celebrity culture
48. My favourite celebrity
49. Profile of a celebrity
50. Celebrities as role models
51. TV reality shows
52. The good and the bad of being famous

Travel and tourism
53. Plans for the holidays
54. Holiday preferences
55. Types of holidays
56. Where to stay
57. Booking accommodation
58. Holiday activities
59. Trips and visits
60. Giving and asking for directions
61. Tourist information
62. Tourist attractions
63. Holiday problems
64. Accommodation problems
65. Eating out
66. Opinions about food
67. The weather

Media and technology
68. Me and my mobile
69. Social media
70. The internet
71. Computer games
72. The good and the bad of technology

The environment and where people live
73. Places in town
74. Things to do
75. Shopping for clothes
76. Transport
77. Travelling on public transport
78. My region – the good and the bad
79. My region in the past
80. Town or country?
81. The environment and me
82. Local environmental issues
83. Global environmental issues
84. Caring for the planet
85. A greener future

About the exams
86. Practice for Paper 1: Listening
87. Practice for Paper 1: Listening
88. Practice for Paper 2: Speaking
89. Practice for Paper 2: Speaking
90. Practice for Paper 3: Reading
91. Practice for Paper 3: Reading
92. Practice for Paper 4: Writing
93. Practice for Paper 4: Writing

Grammar
94. Nouns and articles
95. Adjectives
96. Possessives and pronouns
97. Comparisons
98. Other adjectives
99. Pronouns
100. The present tense
101. Reflexive verbs
102. Irregular verbs (present)
103. *Ser* and *estar*
104. The gerund / present participle
105. The preterite tense
106. The imperfect tense
107. The future tense
108. The conditional tense
109. The perfect tense
110. Giving instructions
111. The present subjunctive
112. Negatives
113. Special verbs
114. *Por* and *para*
115. Asking questions
116. The passive
117. Numbers

Practice papers
118. Paper 1: Listening (Foundation)
121. Paper 2: Speaking (Foundation)
122. Paper 3: Reading (Foundation)
128. Paper 4: Writing (Foundation)
129. Paper 1: Listening (Higher)
133. Paper 2: Speaking (Higher)
134. Paper 3: Reading (Higher)
140. Paper 4: Writing (Higher)

141. Answers

A small bit of small print

AQA publishes Sample Assessment Material and the Specification on its website. This is the official content and this book should be used in conjunction with it. The questions in this Workbook have been written to help you practise every topic in the book. Remember: the real exam questions may not look like this.

1-to-1 page match with the Spanish Revision Guide ISBN 9781292471693

Had a go ☐ **Nearly there** ☐ **Nailed it!** ☐

Identity and relationships with others

Introducing yourself

A message from a new Spanish friend

1 You read this text message.

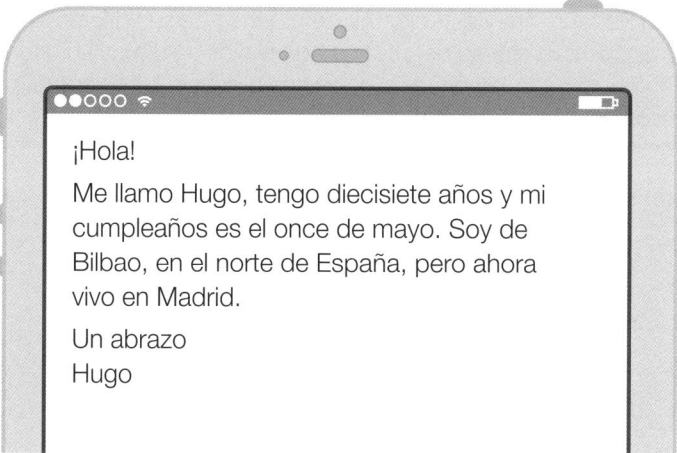

¡Hola!
Me llamo Hugo, tengo diecisiete años y mi cumpleaños es el once de mayo. Soy de Bilbao, en el norte de España, pero ahora vivo en Madrid.
Un abrazo
Hugo

> Be careful not to confuse numbers. Make sure you know the difference between *dieciséis* (16) and *diecisiete* (17).
>
> Also, don't be misled by the word *once* which means 'eleven' (and has nothing to do with the word 'one'!).

Write the **three** correct letters in the boxes.

Hugo …

A	is sixteen.
B	will be eighteen in May.
C	was born on 1 May.
D	is from Bilbao.
E	comes from northern Spain.
F	used to live in Madrid.

(3 marks)

Birthdays

2 Manuel, Nadia and Jorge are talking about themselves.

Answer the questions in **English**.

(a) In which month is Manuel's birthday? .... **(1 mark)**

(b) Where does Nadia live? .... **(1 mark)**

(c) When is Jorge's birthday? .... **(1 mark)**

Listen to the recording

1

Identity and relationships with others

Had a go ☐ Nearly there ☐ Nailed it! ☐

Physical descriptions

In my class

1 You read Natalia's account of the students in her class.

> Voy a un instituto internacional en España y hay estudiantes de muchos países diferentes. Muchos tienen el pelo marrón, hay unos pocos con el pelo negro, tres son rubios y solo hay una chica con pelo rojo. Los chicos que tienen el pelo rubio tienen los ojos azules o grises. La chica del pelo rojo tiene los ojos verdes y muy bonitos. Hay siete en total que llevan gafas.

Complete these sentences. Write the letter for the correct option in each box.

(a) Many students have …

A	black hair.
B	brown hair.
C	blond hair.

(1 mark)

(b) There are … fair-haired students.

A	three
B	five
C	seven

(1 mark)

(c) The student with red hair has …

A	blue eyes.
B	brown eyes.
C	green eyes.

(1 mark)

(d) None of the fair-haired students has …

A	brown eyes.
B	blue eyes.
C	grey eyes.

(1 mark)

Appearances

2 You hear these people talking about the aspects of their appearance that they like and dislike.

Complete the following sentences in **English**.

(a) Martín likes being ………………… but hates his ………………… . (2 marks)

(b) Sara likes her ………………… but not her ………………… . (2 marks)

(c) Álvaro likes his ………………… but thinks he is ………………… . (2 marks)

(d) Andrea likes being ………………… but doesn't like her ………………… . (2 marks)

Listen to the recording

> You won't always hear the verb *gustar* when people are talking about their likes and dislikes. They could use other ways to express their preferences including *me encanta(n)*, or verbs like *odiar*.

2

Had a go ☐ Nearly there ☐ Nailed it! ☐   **Identity and relationships with others**

Character descriptions

A new TV series

1 You read this description of a new Spanish children's programme.

> **Una nueva serie de televisión**
>
> El martes empieza una nueva serie sobre las aventuras de cuatro chicos y su perro.
>
> Alejandro, el chico mayor, es serio y responsable y le gusta ser el jefe del grupo. La chica mayor se llama Begoña y le gustan las actividades deportivas. Al final del día siempre está un poco cansada porque hace mucho ejercicio. Luego está Carlos, un chico simpático y tranquilo, muy popular con los otros porque siempre está contento de ayudarles. La más joven se llama Daniela, una chica alegre y divertida con una actitud positiva.

Answer the following questions.

Write **A** for Alejandro

   B for Begoña

   C for Carlos

   D for Daniela.

Write the correct letter in each box.

Who …

(a)	… is the most helpful?		(d)	… is the natural leader?	
(b)	… is the youngest?		(e)	… has a positive outlook?	
(c)	… always gets tired?		(f)	… is the sporty one?	

(6 marks)

Translation

2 Translate the following sentences into **Spanish**.

I would like to be hard-working and responsible.

....

I am not very sporty, but I am cheerful.

....

I think that I am friendly and fun, with a positive and optimistic attitude.

....

My friends say that I am clever.

....

I went to my friend's house last week and we had a good time.

....

(10 marks)

Identity and relationships with others

Had a go ☐   Nearly there ☐   Nailed it! ☐

Family

Paula's family

1   You read an email from Paula about her family.

> ✉
>
> ¡Hola!
> Antes de visitarnos en abril, necesitas saber un poco sobre la familia con quien vas a vivir. Mis padres, Sebastián y Rosalía, son de un pueblo en el sur de Argentina, pero viven aquí en Málaga desde hace casi veinte años. Tengo un hermano menor, Marcos, que es muy activo y me molesta mucho. Mi hermana mayor se llama Sofía. Es alta y bonita con el pelo largo y negro y los ojos grandes y azules. Desafortunadamente, ¡no me parezco nada a ella! Sofía tiene veintidós años y vive con su pareja en el centro de la ciudad. Mis abuelos viven en una casa muy cerca con nuestra tía Elena, que nunca se casó.
> Un abrazo
> Paula

What does Paula say? Write the **three** correct letters in the boxes.

A	Paula's parents come from northern Argentina.
B	They moved to Málaga nearly 20 years ago.
C	Marcos is annoying.
D	Paula looks a lot like her sister.
E	Sofía got married when she was 22.
F	Paula's aunt Elena is not married.

Each of the statements in the answer options grid contains a key word that is your starting point when searching for the answer in the text. Start with: Argentina, Málaga, Marcos, sister, 22 and Elena and read around the word to find the answer.

☐ ☐ ☐

(3 marks)

Photo card

2   Talk about the content of these photos. You must say at least one thing about each photo.

(5 marks)

After you have spoken about the content of the photos, listen to the recording of further questions on the same topic. Pause the recording to give your answers. There is a sample recording in the Answers section to give you more ideas.

(20 marks)

Had a go ☐ Nearly there ☐ Nailed it! ☐

Identity and relationships with others

What makes a good friend

Reading aloud

1 Read aloud the following text in **Spanish**.

> Mi mejor amiga siempre está allí cuando la necesito.
> Es simpática y tenemos mucho en común.
> Me escucha y me acepta, pero no le importa decirme la verdad.
> Compartimos los mismos intereses en música y vamos a conciertos juntas.
> Es una chica graciosa que me hace reír todo el tiempo.

(5 marks)

> When 'c' is followed by 'a', 'o' or 'u' it has a sound like 'k' in 'kiss' (*música, común, escucha*). When it is followed by 'e' or 'i' it has a sound like 'th' in 'thin' (*graciosa, necesito*).
>
> If 'c' is followed by 'u' and another vowel (*cuando*) it forms a sound like 'kw'.
>
> The combination of 'ch' is like the English 'ch' in 'chat'.

Listen to the recording

Once you have read the text aloud, listen to the four recorded questions related to what you have read. Pause the recording after each one to give yourself time to answer.

In order to score the highest marks, you must try to answer all four questions as fully as you can.

(10 marks)

> After you have read the passage in the exam you will be able to keep the card during the follow-up questions so you can use some of the vocabulary from the passage if you wish.
>
> The questions will be on the same topic. They will include inviting you to talk about or describe something and asking for your opinion on something.
>
> All questions will be in the present tense.

Translation

2 Translate these sentences into **English**.

Mi mejor amiga me ayuda mucho.

....

Me gusta pensar que soy un buen amigo.

....

Un amigo perfecto siempre te acepta como eres.

....

La amistad es muy importante para los jóvenes.

....

Hay momentos cuando tu amigo necesita decirte la verdad.

....

(10 marks)

5

Identity and relationships with others

Had a go ☐ Nearly there ☐ Nailed it! ☐

Relationships

Family relationships

1 You read these comments on an internet forum.

> **Ana:** Cuando era pequeña, me peleaba mucho con mi hermana mayor. Pero cuando empecé a ir al instituto, ella me cuidaba y me protegía de las chicas mayores que no eran muy simpáticas.
>
> **Bruno:** Estoy muy enojado con mis padres porque a mi hermano y a mí nos tratan diferente. Él tiene mucha más libertad que yo y, en mi opinión, esto no es justo. Deberían tratarnos con igualdad.
>
> **Cris:** Tengo que compartir un dormitorio con mi hermano menor y me molesta mucho. Siempre hace ruido cuando intento estudiar y terminamos discutiendo todo el tiempo. Necesito mi propio espacio.

Answer the following questions.

Write   **A** for Ana
       B for Bruno
       C for Cris.

> Remember that, unlike other question styles, these questions do not follow the same order as the texts. You have to read each person's comment to find the answers.

Write the correct letter in each box.

Who …

(a)	… wants more freedom?	☐
(b)	… needs their own space?	☐
(c)	… used to fight a lot?	☐
(d)	… is always arguing?	☐
(e)	… was protected at school?	☐
(f)	… thinks their parents are unfair?	☐

(6 marks)

Your friends

2 Write an article about your friends.

Write approximately **50** words in **Spanish**. You must write something about each bullet point.

Mention:
- what your best friend looks like
- your best friend's personality
- activities with your friends
- an aspect you do not like about a friend
- what sort of a friend you are.

> Don't think that you need to write lots to score good marks. Stick to the word recommendation and aim for quality not quantity.

(10 marks)

....
....
....
....

Had a go ☐   Nearly there ☐   Nailed it! ☐   **Identity and relationships with others**

Helping a friend

Dictation

1 You will hear five short sentences.

Listen carefully and using your knowledge of Spanish sounds, write down in **Spanish** exactly what you hear for each sentence. You will hear each sentence **three** times: the first time as a full sentence, the second time in short sections and the third time again as a full sentence.

Sentence 1

....

Sentence 2

....

Sentence 3

....

Sentence 4

....

Sentence 5

....

(10 marks)

Remember that you hear each sentence three times. Each sentence will be between five and seven words. Make sure your writing is really clear and, if you want to change a word, put a clear line through it and write the new word above.

In the exam, the different sentences may be on any topic, but here you are practising the topic **Identity and relationship with others**.

Photo card

2 Talk about the content of these photos. You must say at least **one** thing about each photo.

(5 marks)

After you have spoken about the content of the photos, listen to the recording of further questions on the same topic. Pause the recording to give your answers. There is a sample recording in the Answers section to give you more ideas.

(20 marks)

Although the photos will be in black and white, it is fine to imagine the colours of things and to describe a 'yellow shirt' or a 'blue T-shirt'.

7

Healthy living and lifestyle

Had a go ☐ Nearly there ☐ Nailed it! ☐

Food and drink

Eating out

1 You read these reviews of a restaurant.

> **Nadia**
> Decidimos no tomar nada de primero, lo que fue una buena decisión porque la paella que compartimos era enorme. Estaba muy rica y el arroz estaba cocinado perfectamente. Después, mi marido tomó una ensalada de frutas, pero yo no pude comer más.
>
> **Emilio**
> Vamos a este restaurante muchas veces porque la calidad de las hamburguesas y los platos de pollo es excelente. Anoche la cena fue tan buena como siempre, pero pienso que los precios han subido bastante recientemente.
>
> **Carmen**
> Ayer mi familia y yo disfrutamos de una tarde muy agradable en mi restaurante favorito, probando las muchas tapas que allí hay. Lo que me gusta más es que preparan el tipo de comida que prefiero – típicamente española y tradicional.

Complete these sentences. Write the letter for the correct option in each box.

(a) Nadia thought the *paella* was …

A	disappointing.
B	huge.
C	under-cooked.

(b) Nadia …

A	had fruit cake for pudding.
B	had fresh fruit for dessert.
C	did not have dessert.

(c) Emilio likes the restaurant because of …

A	the quality of the fish.
B	how good the meat is.
C	the vegetarian options.

(d) Carmen's favourite type of food is …

A	a mixture of international cuisine.
B	different dishes of tapas.
C	traditional Spanish cooking.

(4 marks)

> Remember that the suffix *-dad* on the end of a Spanish word is the equivalent of *-ty* on the end of an English word. So it is possible to work out that *calidad* = quality.

An article

2 You are writing an article about food.

Write approximately **90** words in **Spanish**.

You must write something about each bullet point.

Mention:

- what you like to eat
- a meal you had recently
- what you are going to make for a special occasion in the future.

> In the exam you will have more space for your writing. Here you can continue on your own paper if necessary.

> Remember the rules about using *gustar*: use *gusta* if what follows is singular, or a verb, and *gustan* if what follows is plural. Also remember to include the article (*el, la, los, las*) with nouns after *gustar*.

....
....
....
....

(15 marks)

Had a go ☐   Nearly there ☐   Nailed it! ☐

Healthy living and lifestyle

Healthy eating

Target grade 1-9

Photo card

1 Talk about the content of these photos. You must say at least one thing about each photo.

(5 marks)

After you have spoken about the content of the photos, listen to the recording of further questions on the same topic. Pause the recording to give your answers. There is a sample recording in the Answers section to give you more ideas.

(20 marks)

> Remember that in the Speaking and Writing exams you can use words that are not on the specified vocabulary list. You can use any of the vocabulary that you know. Here it would be fine if you mentioned that there are lots of *fresas* (strawberries) on the table.

> Keep in mind that although the photos will be in black and white, it is fine to imagine the colours of things and to describe them.

Target grade 1-5

Reading aloud

2 Read aloud the following text in **Spanish**.

> Normalmente tomo un huevo para el desayuno.
> A veces como un poco de pan.
> Evito la comida rápida como las hamburguesas.
> Sin embargo, me gustan los bocadillos de jamón.
> También me encantan las manzanas y las uvas.

(5 marks)

Once you have read the text aloud, listen to the four recorded questions related to what you have read. Pause the recording after each one to give yourself time to answer.

In order to score the highest marks, you must try to answer all four questions as fully as you can.

(10 marks)

> You can hear a recording of the text and sample answers in the Answers section.

> Remember that the second u in *hamburguesa* is not pronounced, so the sound is like the 'ge' in 'get' and not the 'Gw' in 'Gwen'.

> Double 'll' (as in *bocadillo*) can be pronounced like the 'li' in mil<u>li</u>on or the 'y' in <u>y</u>ellow.

Healthy living and lifestyle

Had a go ☐ Nearly there ☐ Nailed it! ☐

Sport and exercise

Getting fit

1 You are listening to María, Jaime and Teresa talking about their favourite activities. What advantage and disadvantage of the activity does each one mention?

Write the correct letter and number in each box.

	Advantage
A	Being one of a team
B	Forgetting your problems
C	Keeping fit
D	Losing weight
E	Spending time outdoors

	Disadvantage
1	Bad weather
2	Can be too busy
3	Constant training
4	Expensive equipment
5	Frequent injuries

	Advantage	Disadvantage	
(a) María	☐	☐	(2 marks)
(b) Jaime	☐	☐	(2 marks)
(c) Teresa	☐	☐	(2 marks)

> Listen out for words like *mejor, bueno, ventaja* for the positive aspects and words like *malo, peor, desventaja* for the negative aspects.

Role play

2 You are talking to your Cuban friend.

Listen to the recording of the teacher's part. The teacher will play the part of your friend and will speak first.

You should address your friend as *tú*.

When you see this – **?** – you will have to ask a question.

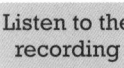

| 1 Say what your favourite sport or exercise is. (Give **one** detail.) |
| 2 Say when you do the activity. (Give **one** detail.) |
| 3 Say who you do the activity with. |
| 4 Say where you do the activity. |
| ?5 Ask your friend a question about sport. |

(10 marks)

> In order to score full marks, you must include a verb in your response to each task.

> The key verbs when you are talking about the sport or exercise that you do are: *juego* (I play), *hago* (I do), *voy* (I go) – when talking about a place you go to – and *monto + en bicicleta / a caballo* (I ride my bike / I go horseriding).

Had a go ☐ Nearly there ☐ Nailed it! ☐

Healthy living and lifestyle

Physical wellbeing

Photo card

1 Talk about the content of these photos. You must say at least one thing about each photo.

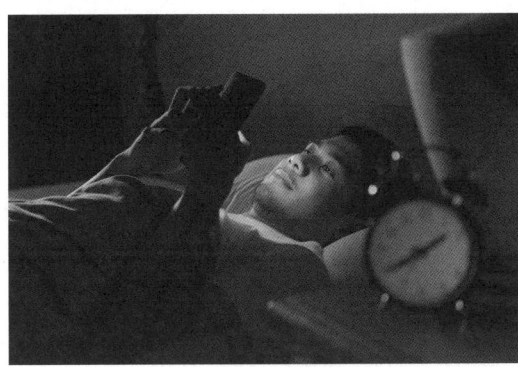

(5 marks)

> During your preparation time, make as many notes as you wish on an Additional Answer Sheet and use these notes during the test. Remember that you are expected to talk for approximately **one and a half minutes** at Higher tier.

After you have spoken about the content of the photos, listen to the recording of further questions on the same topic. Pause the recording to give your answers. There is a sample recording in the Answers section to give you more ideas.

(20 marks)

Translation

2 Translate the following sentences into **Spanish**.

My brother sleeps very well every night.

....
....

I like to spend time in the open air.

....
....

I drank lots of water yesterday.

....
....

The sun can do damage to your skin.

....
....

She is very tired today.

....
....

(10 marks)

11

Healthy living and lifestyle

Had a go ☐ Nearly there ☐ Nailed it! ☐

Mental wellbeing

Target grade 6-7

Listen to the recording

Looking after your mental wellbeing

1 David, Alba and Luis are talking about mental wellbeing. What do they say?

Write the correct letter in each box.

(a) David thinks you shouldn't spend all the time …

A	on school work.
B	worrying.
C	relaxing.

(b) He unwinds by …

A	playing sport.
B	going out with friends.
C	watching a match.

(c) In the past, at school, Alba felt …

A	bullied.
B	she was failing.
C	ill with stress.

(d) Alba's sister helps …

A	with Alba's homework.
B	by listening.
C	because she gives good advice.

(e) Luis says he …

A	never gets upset.
B	very often gets anxious.
C	is occasionally sad.

(f) He lets out his emotions …

A	when he sings on stage.
B	in the lyrics he writes.
C	through listening to music.

(6 marks)

> The alternative options in multiple choice questions often use vocabulary that you will hear in the recording. You are listening for detail and not the general gist. Careful listening will allow you to reject the wrong answers and arrive at the correct one.

Target grade 1-5

Translation

> The *me* in sentence 2 needs to be translated – it is the object of the verb for which *abuelo* is the subject. However, the *me* in sentence 3 does not need to be put into English because *sentirse* is a reflexive verb in Spanish, but 'to feel' is not reflexive in English.

2 Translate these sentences into **English**.

Me gusta pintar porque es muy fácil.

....

....

Mi abuelo siempre me escucha.

....

....

Cuando me siento triste, hablo con mis amigos.

....

....

Ayudé a mi hermano cuando tenía un problema.

....

....

La familia es muy importante en mi vida.

....

....

(10 marks)

Had a go ☐ Nearly there ☐ Nailed it! ☐

Healthy living and lifestyle

Role models in sport

Changes in sport

1 You read this article about women's football.

> En 2022 vimos el primer partido de fútbol masculino* en una Copa del Mundo con una mujer, la francesa Stéphanie Frappart, como árbitra**. Estaba muy contenta cuando vi este partido porque además de tener una mujer como árbitra, también había dos mujeres de otros países como juezas de línea*** – una **brasileña** y una mexicana. Cuando yo era joven, las chicas simplemente no jugaban al fútbol; no estaba permitido. Solo nos dejaban jugar al tenis o al hockey ¡pero nunca con los chicos! Cada día hay más igualdad en el deporte, pero todavía hay mucho por hacer.

**el fútbol masculino* – men's football   **la árbitra – female referee
****la jueza de línea* – line judge, assistant referee

Answer the following questions in **English**.

(a) Why did Stéphanie Frappart make the headlines in 2022?

.... **(1 mark)**

(b) What else was remarkable about the match?

.... **(1 mark)**

(c) What does the writer say about football for girls when she was young?

.... **(1 mark)**

(d) What does she say about equality in sport in the modern day?

.... **(1 mark)**

(e) Read the second sentence again. What does the word *brasileña* refer to? Write the correct letter in the box.

A	a football position
B	a nationality
C	an award

☐ **(1 mark)**

Translation

2 Translate the following sentences into **Spanish**.

I play for the football team in my school.

....

I love sport because it helps me to keep fit.

....

I enjoy the friendship with the team members.

....

Last week we won a match against a school from another town.

....

This Saturday I think we will lose against a very good team.

....

(10 marks)

Healthy living and lifestyle

Had a go ☐   Nearly there ☐   Nailed it! ☐

Sporting events

Sporting events

1 You read three social media comments about sporting events.

> **A:** La semana pasada fui con mi familia a ver un partido de fútbol en el estadio de la ciudad. Desafortunadamente, no estuvimos cómodos porque llovió y tuvimos bastante frío.
> *Alicia*
>
> **B:** Anoche mi prima jugó en un partido de baloncesto en el centro de deportes. Había mucha gente allí y tuvimos una experiencia estupenda porque el ambiente fue muy emocionante.
> *Benjamín*
>
> **C:** Ayer mi hermano nadó en un concurso y fuimos a la piscina para ver la competición. Pasamos una tarde agradable porque mi hermano ganó varias carreras.
> *Claudia*

Which opinion matches each description?

Write the correct letter in each box.

(a) Family success ☐ **(1 mark)**

(b) Bad weather ☐ **(1 mark)**

(c) Exciting atmosphere ☐ **(1 mark)**

Photo card

2 Talk about the content of these photos. You must say at least one thing about each photo.

(5 marks)

Listen to the recording

After you have spoken about the content of the photos, listen to the recording of further questions on the same topic. Pause the recording to give your answers. **(20 marks)**

> There is a sample answer from a student working at around Grade 5 in the Answers section.

Had a go ☐ Nearly there ☐ Nailed it! ☐

Education and work

School subjects

Class teachers

1 You hear these teachers talking in class. Which subjects are being taught? Write the correct letter in each box.

Listen to the recording

(a) The first teacher is teaching …

A	Art.
B	Geography.
C	History.

> The subject is not mentioned by name but there are clues in what each teacher says that will lead you to the correct answer.

(1 mark)

(b) The second teacher is teaching …

A	Science.
B	Religious Studies.
C	P.E.

(1 mark)

(c) The third teacher is teaching …

A	Maths.
B	English.
C	Music.

(1 mark)

Reading aloud

2 Read aloud the following text in **Spanish**.

> Actualmente estudio varias asignaturas.
> Pronto tengo que escoger las que quiero hacer el año próximo.
> Me gustan las lenguas, y pienso continuar con el inglés.
> Saco buenas notas en matemáticas, pero la clase de educación física es mi favorita.
> Voy a dejar la historia porque nunca puedo aprender las fechas.

(5 marks)

Listen to the recording

Once you have read the text aloud, listen to the four recorded questions related to what you have read. Pause the recording after each one to give yourself time to answer.

In order to score the highest marks, you must try to answer all four questions as fully as you can.

(10 marks)

> You can check your reading by listening to a recording of the text in the Answers section. You can also hear sample answers to the questions.

> Remember to pronounce the letter 'v' as if it were a 'b' (in *voy* and *varias*). When Spanish children learn to write they often make the mistake of spelling these words with an intial 'b' because of the pronunciation.
>
> Listen to and repeat these words: *voy, varias, viernes, visto*.
>
> The letter 'h' is silent unless it is combined with 'c' as in 'ch' (pronounced like 'ch' in 'church').
>
> Listen to and repeat these words: *hermano, historia, hotel, dicho, fecha, escuchar*.

Track 16

Education and work

Had a go ☐   Nearly there ☐   Nailed it! ☐

School subjects – likes and dislikes

Listen to the recording

Dictation

1 You will hear five short sentences.

Listen carefully and using your knowledge of Spanish sounds, write down in **Spanish** exactly what you hear for each sentence. You will hear each sentence **three** times: the first time as a full sentence, the second time in short sections and the third time again as a full sentence.

Sentence 1

....

Sentence 2

....

Sentence 3

....

Sentence 4

....

Sentence 5

....

(10 marks)

> In the exam, the different sentences may be on any topic, but here you are practising the topic **Education and work**.

A letter about school

2 You are writing a letter to your friend about your school subjects.

Write approximately **90** words in **Spanish**.

You must write something about each bullet point.

Mention:

- your opinion of one of your subjects with reasons
- what subjects you dropped in the past
- what you will study next year.

> To achieve the top band of marks, you need to address all the bullet points, develop your ideas and show some variety of vocabulary and phrases. A good way of extending your points is to express the reasons you do/did something even when the bullet point does not specifically require you to do so (such as the last two bullet points in this task).

....

....

....

....

....

....

....

(15 marks)

Had a go ☐ Nearly there ☐ Nailed it! ☐

Education and work

The school day

Secondary school

1 You read these comments on an internet forum.

> **Andrea:** Mi colegio está bastante lejos y tengo que ir en autobús. Es un problema porque no puedo participar en las actividades después de las clases porque tengo que coger el autobús.
>
> **Bruno:** En mi instituto, tenemos una hora para comer y las clases terminan a las cuatro menos diez. Preferiría continuar sin parar y terminar antes.
>
> **Cris:** Durante el recreo, nos gusta salir al patio al aire libre. Allí hablamos con los amigos y comemos un bocadillo. Pero no hay ningún sitio para descansar. El instituto necesita poner unas mesas y sillas en el patio.

Who says what?

Write **A** for Andrea

   B for Bruno

   C for Cris.

Write the correct letter in each box.

Who …

(a)	… has a long lunch hour?	
(b)	… can't walk to school?	
(c)	… has a snack at break?	
(d)	… wants better facilities outside?	
(e)	… can't join in the school clubs?	
(f)	… wants to shorten the school day?	

(6 marks)

An email about the school day

2 You are writing an email to your friend about the school day.

Write approximately **90** words in **Spanish**.

You must write something about each bullet point.

Mention:

- when classes start and finish
- how you went to school last week
- what lessons you are going to have tomorrow.

> Continue your answer on your own paper if you run out of space here.

> It does not matter if you write a lot about one bullet point and a lot less on another one. In this task, the first bullet point could be answered briefly if you have a lot more to say about the second, for example. As long as you answer all points, the balance does not matter.

……………………………………………………………………………………………………
……………………………………………………………………………………………………
……………………………………………………………………………………………………
……………………………………………………………………………………………………
……………………………………………………………………………………………………
……………………………………………………………………………………………………

(15 marks)

Education and work

Had a go ☐ Nearly there ☐ Nailed it! ☐

School facilities

School facilities

1. You read these comments from students about the school's facilities.

> **Elena:** Me gusta el instituto porque el gimnasio es muy moderno y tenemos muchos ordenadores.
>
> **Daniel:** Me parece que tenemos una biblioteca excelente, con muchos libros y espacio para estudiar. Sin embargo, el patio del instituto es demasiado pequeño.
>
> **Laura:** Gracias al instituto por organizar los viajes y las excursiones – son una oportunidad increíble.

What opinion do they express about their school?

Write **P** for a **positive** opinion

N for a **negative** opinion

P+N for a **positive** and **negative** opinion.

Write the correct letter in each box.

(a) Elena ☐ **(1 mark)**

(b) Daniel ☐ **(1 mark)**

(c) Laura ☐ **(1 mark)**

Picture task

2. You decide to send this photo on WhatsApp to a friend in Argentina.

What is in this photo?

Write **five** sentences in **Spanish**.

....

....

....

....

.... **(10 marks)**

> There is a lot you could say about this picture – plenty of choice. You can describe the people and their clothes, mention the things they are using, explain the activities that they are doing (like writing and looking for information on the internet) and you can talk about where they are and what it is like.

Had a go ☐   Nearly there ☐   Nailed it! ☐

Education and work

School uniform

Photo card

1 Talk about the content of these photos. You must say at least one thing about each photo.

(5 marks)

After you have spoken about the content of the photos, listen to the recording of further questions on the same topic. Pause the recording to give your answers. There is a sample recording in the Answers section to give you more ideas. **(20 marks)**

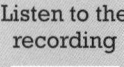

> Remember that you can use words that are not on the prescribed AQA vocabulary list. When describing your school uniform you can use words like *la chaqueta* ('jacket', 'blazer'), *la corbata* ('tie') and *el jersey* ('jumper') as well as other words for clothing that are on the list.

School uniform

2 You listen to Emilio, Marta and Hugo talking about school uniform.

What do they say? Write the correct letter in each box.

(a) Emilio thinks …

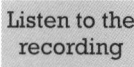

A	their uniform is very unpopular.
B	all school uniforms should be the same.
C	students should have a say in the uniform colour.

☐ **(1 mark)**

(b) Marta says …

A	all schools ought to have a uniform.
B	buying a uniform is too expensive.
C	they should sell second-hand uniform in schools.

☐ **(1 mark)**

(c) Hugo …

A	says that not having uniform leads to discrimination.
B	worries about families who can't afford the uniform.
C	does not see any connection between uniform and equality.

☐ **(1 mark)**

> As well as the five minutes of reading time at the start of the exam, there is also a pause after the question number is announced. This gives you a moment to glance over the question again and remind yourself of the scenario and the question style.

Education and work

Had a go ☐ Nearly there ☐ Nailed it! ☐

Activities in class

Reading aloud

1 Read aloud the following text in **Spanish**.

> Me gustan más las clases de educación física porque soy una persona activa.
> Primero hacemos ejercicio en el gimnasio nuevo.
> Luego salimos al campo de deportes para jugar al fútbol o al baloncesto.
> No me interesan nada las clases de historia.
> Tenemos que escuchar, leer y escribir todo el tiempo.

(5 marks)

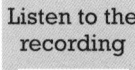

Once you have read the text aloud, listen to the four recorded questions related to what you have read. Pause the recording after each one to give yourself time to answer.

In order to score the highest marks, you must try to answer all four questions as fully as you can.

(10 marks)

You can hear a sample recording of the text, questions and answers in the Answers section.

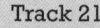

Track 21

Remember that the letter 'j' and the letter 'g' (when followed by 'e' or 'i') are pronounced like the 'ch' in the Scottish word 'loch'. (The 'j' sound like in the English word 'jump' does not exist in Spanish).

When you see a tricky word like *ejercicio* in a read aloud task, say it over silently in your head a few times during the preparation time to familiarise yourself with its pronunciation.

Play the recording to listen to the following words. Repeat the words to practise the sound:

dejar, mejor, juntos, jardín

región, alérgico, colegio

general, proteger, gente

School classes

2 You are writing to your friend about your classes at school.

Write approximately **90** words in **Spanish**.

You must write something about each bullet point.

Mention:

- what your timetable is like
- what you did in one of your lessons last week
- what you are going to do in a different class next week.

Continue your answer on your own paper if you run out of space here.

Ensure that you don't repeat yourself. Bullet points 2 and 3 are about class activities so make sure you talk about different things for each one and don't use the same vocabulary.

....
....
....
....
....

(15 marks)

Had a go ☐ **Nearly there** ☐ **Nailed it!** ☐

Education and work

School rules

Dictation

1 You will hear four short sentences. Listen carefully and using your knowledge of Spanish sounds, write down in **Spanish** exactly what you hear for each sentence. You will hear each sentence **three** times: the first time as a full sentence, the second time in short sections and the third time again as a full sentence.

Sentence 1

....

Sentence 2

....

Sentence 3

....

Sentence 4

....

(8 marks)

> If you can understand the sentences, it will help you even more to write the words with the correct spellings. So, use your understanding of the Spanish language to guide you. For instance, after *las* ('the') in the first sentence, the next word must be a feminine plural noun.
>
> You can sometimes use your knowledge of the English language to help. For example, in sentence 4, you will hear the Spanish for 'prohibited'. Your knowledge of the English word will remind you that there is a silent letter 'h' in the Spanish word.

Translation

2 Translate the following sentences into **Spanish**.

You must do your homework every day.

....

You must not drop litter in the playground.

....

You cannot bring your mobile to class.

....

We must always have the necessary equipment.

....

My friend arrived late to school yesterday.

....

(10 marks)

> When translating 'your homework' or 'your mobile', the best way is to simply use the article (*los deberes*, *el móvil*). In Spanish it seems obvious that it must be yours, so it isn't felt necessary to say so.
>
> With 'school' and 'class', you leave out the article 'the' in English, but it is always included in Spanish (*el instituto / colegio* and *la clase*).

Education and work

Had a go ☐ Nearly there ☐ Nailed it! ☐

The good and the bad about school

A blog about school

1 You read Nadia's blog about school.

> El sitio que más me gusta de mi instituto es la biblioteca. Tiene muchos ordenadores nuevos. Un problema con mi instituto es el horario. Empezamos a las ocho – es demasiado temprano.

Answer the questions in **English**. You do not need to write in full sentences.

(a) Which place in school does Nadia like best? .... **(1 mark)**

(b) Why does she like it? .... **(1 mark)**

(c) What problem does she mention? .... **(1 mark)**

(d) Why is it a problem? .... **(1 mark)**

> Remember that the questions follow the order of the text. Knowing this helps you locate the correct information in the text.

Translation

2 Translate the following sentences into **Spanish**.

The head teacher is very fair.

....

I passed the exam last week.

....

We can ask for help in class.

....

Something that I like a lot is the use of technology.

....

Some teachers give us too much homework.

....

(10 marks)

> In the Foundation translation, you can expect four sentences to be in the present tense and one or two to be either in the past tense or the future. The past tense sentence here is sentence 2: the verb *aprobar* ('to pass') is regular in the preterite tense. Also, be careful with the verb 'to ask <u>for</u>'. Clue: it is one word and it isn't *preguntar*.

Had a go ☐ Nearly there ☐ Nailed it! ☐

Education and work

School clubs and activities

School clubs

1 You read Gabriela's account of her favourite school club.

> Cada jueves, en el instituto, voy al Club de Cultura Española que organiza nuestra profesora de castellano*. Dura tres cuartos de hora y cada semana hay un evento diferente. A veces la profesora nos hace una presentación con fotos sobre distintos aspectos del país. Hoy hemos escuchado canciones y disfruté leyendo la letra. De vez en cuando, uno de los estudiantes con más experiencia presenta un proyecto sobre un tema relacionado con España o Sudamérica. La semana próxima, vamos a probar unas tapas. Todos los estudiantes que participan en el club van a traer algo que han hecho en casa.

* Spanish language

Complete these sentences. Write the letter for the correct option in each box.

(a) The club on Thursdays is organised by …

A	the Cultural centre.
B	the language students.
C	the Spanish teacher.

(b) The sessions last …

A	an hour.
B	forty-five minutes.
C	half an hour.

(c) The teacher tells them …

A	how to improve their language.
B	about Spanish music.
C	different things about the country.

(d) Today in the club, Gabriela …

A	enjoyed reading song lyrics.
B	had fun singing in Spanish.
C	tried to write a song.

(e) Sometimes, the club is run by …

A	a visiting speaker.
B	an older student.
C	a Spanish-speaking parent.

(f) Next week, they will be …

A	sampling food.
B	watching a film.
C	learning about customs.

(6 marks)

After-school clubs

2 Sofía is talking about after-school clubs.

Answer the questions in **English**.

(a) When did Sofía learn about English schools?

.... **(1 mark)**

(b) When did most activities take place?

.... **(1 mark)**

(c) What kind of classes does she say you can attend in Spain? Mention **two**.

.... **(2 marks)**

(d) Why are these activities different from the ones organised in England? Give **two** reasons.

.... **(2 marks)**

Education and work

Had a go ☐ Nearly there ☐ Nailed it! ☐

How to be a good student

Exam preparation podcast

1 You hear Hugo's podcast about preparing for exams. What does he say?

   Write the **three** correct letters in the boxes.

A	You need to make a study plan.
B	Re-reading the text book is the best thing to do.
C	Doing something active is a good study method.
D	Having regular healthy meals is important.
E	Write important dates on paper to stick to your wall.
F	Don't forget to take regular breaks.

Listen to the recording

(3 marks)

Photo card

2 Talk about the content of these photos. You must say at least one thing about each photo.

(5 marks)

Listen to the recording

After you have spoken about the content of the photos, listen to the recording of further questions on the same topic. Pause the recording to give your answers. There is a sample recording in the Answers section to give you more ideas.

(20 marks)

> When planning your response to the photo card, always use language that you are sure you know the Spanish for. Don't make up words!
>
> When you have finished your description, play the recording to hear and respond to the sort of questions you may be asked in the conversation that follows your description of the photos.

Had a go ☐ **Nearly there** ☐ **Nailed it!** ☐

Education and work

Options at 16

Careers Day

1 You listen to a head teacher explaining about Careers Day in school.

What do they say? Write the correct letter in each box.

(a) Because of Careers Day, they have cancelled …

A	all lessons.
B	Science lessons.
C	P.E. lessons.

(1 mark)

(b) You need to ask the teachers for information if …

A	you want to take up a new subject.
B	you are unsure of your grades.
C	you are thinking of changing schools.

(1 mark)

(c) You should go to the library for information on …

A	university application.
B	part-time jobs.
C	vocational qualifications.

(1 mark)

(d) You should go to the technology classroom to hear about …

A	going to a local college.
B	chances to study abroad.
C	work experience opportunities.

(1 mark)

> *Carrera* can be a career, a university course or a race. It usually depends on the context to make it clear. A *título* is a qualification, sometimes implying a university qualification or degree.

Reading aloud

2 Read aloud the following text in **Spanish**.

> El año próximo voy a seguir estudiando en el instituto.
> Sin embargo, no estoy segura de qué voy a escoger.
> Me gustan las ciencias.
> También las matemáticas son muy útiles.
> Mi decisión depende de mis notas.

(5 marks)

Once you have read the text aloud, listen to the **four** recorded questions related to what you have read. Pause the recording after each one to give yourself time to answer.

In order to score the highest marks, you must try to answer all **four** questions as fully as you can.

(10 marks)

> When you read the word *instituto*, remember that the 't' sound is very pure and not at all like the 'choo' sound we make in English when we say 'insti**tu**te' or '**tu**tor'.
>
> Listen to these words, with the same 'tu' sound being pronounced:
>
> *futuro, aventura, temperatura, instituto*

Track 28

25

Education and work

Had a go ☐ Nearly there ☐ Nailed it! ☐

Future study plans

A college visit

1 You listen to Natalia and Juan talking about the college they are visiting.

Answer the following questions in **English**.

Listen to the recording

(a) What has impressed Natalia about the college?

.... (1 mark)

(b) What is the disadvantage of the college for her?

.... (1 mark)

(c) What has impressed Juan about the college?

.... (1 mark)

(d) What is he not so keen on?

.... (1 mark)

> The information you need for the answers comes in the same order as the questions. So you will first hear Natalia speak; she will start by mentioning what she likes and will then talk about what she does not like. The same will then happen with Juan.

General conversation

2 After the Photo card in the exam, you won't see the general conversation questions written down, you will only hear your teacher asking them.

Listen to the recording

Here are some typical questions on the topic of **Future study plans**. Think about how you would answer them. Then play the recording of the questions and pause the recording after each question to give your answer.

- ¿Qué planes tienes para tus estudios el año próximo?
- ¿Cuáles son tus razones para escoger este curso?
- ¿Quieres ir a la universidad?
- ¿Cuáles son los beneficios de ir a la universidad?
- ¿Cuáles son los aspectos negativos?
- ¿Qué otras cosas te gustaría aprender en el futuro?

> Your answers should be easily comprehensible and relevant to the questions. Your ideas should be developed through extended sequences of speech, you should aim for a wide and accurate range of vocabulary and grammar, and include references to past, present and future.

Had a go ☐ Nearly there ☐ Nailed it! ☐

Education and work

Future plans

Dictation

Listen to the recording

1. You will hear five short sentences. Listen carefully and using your knowledge of Spanish sounds, write down in **Spanish** exactly what you hear for each sentence. You will hear each sentence **three** times: the first time as a full sentence, the second time in short sections and the third time again as a full sentence.

Sentence 1

....

Sentence 2

....

Sentence 3

....

Sentence 4

....

Sentence 5

....

(10 marks)

> Words like *farmacia* are not stressed on the letter 'i', so there is no accent on the 'i'. On words like *sería* (*ser* in the conditional tense) the letter 'i' is stressed therefore an accent is needed. Try to apply this rule to the three words in this category in the dictation.

A blog about your plans

2. You are writing a blog about your studies and future plans.

   Write approximately **150** words in **Spanish**.

   You must write something about both bullet points.

   Mention:
   • your current studies
   • your future plans for education and work.

> On the Higher writing paper, one of the bullet points in question 3 will either be in the past or future tense. Here you are asked about the future so will need to use future tenses and verbs in the present that communicate future plans like *Espero* + infinitive ('I hope to …') and *Quiero* + infinitive ('I want to …').

....

....

....

....

....

....

....

....

....

(25 marks)

Education and work

Had a go ☐   Nearly there ☐   Nailed it! ☐

Part-time jobs and money

Starting a new job

1 Julia is about to start a new part-time job. You hear her talking about it.

Answer the following questions in **English**.

(a) What day will she be working? .... (1 mark)

(b) Where exactly will she be working? Give **two** details.

....

.... (2 marks)

(c) What is she going to do tomorrow? .... (1 mark)

(d) What time will she normally start? .... (1 mark)

> In questions (a) and (c) you need to listen carefully as you will hear two possible answers (e.g. two different days and two different times). You need to pay close attention in order to eliminate the wrong answer and select the correct one.

Picture task

2 You decide to send this photo on WhatsApp to a friend in Spain.

What is in this photo? Write **five** sentences in **Spanish**.

....

....

....

....

.... (10 marks)

> This is the first question on the Foundation writing paper, allowing you to give straightforward pieces of information about any aspect of the photo. Your sentences just need to be relevant to the photo and communicate a clear message.

Had a go ☐ Nearly there ☐ Nailed it! ☐   **Education and work**

Opinions about jobs

A job forum

1 Read the comments and queries on an internet forum.

> **Pilar:** Me gustaría ser profesora de niños pequeños. ¿Cuántos años de estudio tienes que hacer en la universidad?
>
> **Andrea:** Me interesa trabajar como policía en el futuro. ¿Me puedes decir cuál es el salario?
>
> **Marcos:** Quisiera trabajar como escritor. ¿Qué asignatura sería mejor estudiar en la universidad?

Who asks about the following issues?

Write **P** for Pilar

A for Andrea

M for Marcos.

Write the correct letter in each box.

Who asks about …

(a)	… being a writer?	
(b)	… choosing a subject?	
(c)	… joining the police?	
(d)	… becoming a teacher?	
(e)	… the length of the course?	
(f)	… the money you earn?	

(6 marks)

Reading aloud

2 Read aloud the following text in **Spanish**.

> Creo que me gustaría ser actriz.
> Sé que es muy difícil encontrar empleo en el cine o la televisión.
> Sin embargo, hay que seguir los sueños.
> Pienso que voy a ir a la universidad para estudiar inglés y teatro.
> Así, tendré un título si no logro conseguir mi trabajo ideal.

(5 marks)

Once you have read the text aloud, listen to the **four** recorded questions related to what you have read. Pause the recording after each one to give yourself time to answer.

In order to score the highest marks, you must try to answer all **four** questions as fully as you can.

(10 marks)

> Be careful when pronouncing 'i' and 'e'. The letter 'i' is always like in *si* or *ir* so it will be the same in *ideal* – do not be tempted to produce the sound 'eye' like in the English word 'ideal'.
>
> You should also hear a total difference in the way you pronounce *mi* and *me*, so when you say *me gustaría*, ensure you say *me* (meh) and not *mi*.
>
> Listen to these examples: *idea, ideal, final, dieta, me gustaría, me llamo, mi casa, mi familia*

Track 34

Education and work

Had a go ☐ Nearly there ☐ Nailed it! ☐

The pros and cons of different jobs

Photo card

1 Talk about the content of these photos. You must say at least **one** thing about each photo.

(5 marks)

After you have spoken about the content of the photos, listen to the recording of further questions on the same topic. Pause the recording to give your answers. There is a sample recording in the Answers section to give you more ideas.

(20 marks)

> With the first picture, you could guess that it is the start of the day, perhaps nine o'clock because the people are arriving in the office or have just arrived (using *acabar de* + infinitive). You could also consider why the man has brought his bike into the office (to keep it safe? – *para mantenerla segura*).

Translation

2 Translate these sentences into **English**.

Quiero trabajar en una oficina con equipo moderno.

....

Hay muchas reglas en esta empresa.

....

Mi hermana espera ser científica o profesora.

....

Fui al extranjero seis veces cuando trabajaba con la compañía.

....

No me gustaría ser médico; es demasiado difícil.

....

(10 marks)

> Be careful with words that have more than one meaning. Think about which meaning makes sense on the context. For example, *equipo* can mean 'team' or 'equipment' and *regla* can mean 'rule' or 'ruler'.

Had a go ☐ **Nearly there** ☐ **Nailed it!** ☐

Education and work

Job adverts

Target grade 1-5

Translation

1 Translate the following sentences into **Spanish**.

I need to call the company.

....

I am hard working and I have a positive attitude.

....

I am looking for information online.

....

My sister found a job in the newspaper.

....

The firm wants people with experience.

....

(10 marks)

> For sentence 3, remember that 'to look for' is *buscar* – *you* do not need an extra word for 'for'. Also, in this sentence you can use the ordinary present (*busco*) or the present continuous (*estoy buscando*).

Target grade 4-9

Listen to the recording

Role play

2 You are talking to a Mexican friend about jobs.

Your teacher will play the part of your friend and will speak first.

You should address your friend as *tú*.

When you see this – **?** – you will have to ask a question.

> 1 Say what sort of job you want. (Give **two** details.)
> 2 Say what talents you have for the job. (Give **two** details.)
> 3 Give **one** opinion about working abroad and give **one** reason.
> 4 Say where you are going to find more information.
> ?5 Ask your friend a question about work.

(10 marks)

> In order to score full marks, you must include a verb in your response to each task.

> The higher role plays always require you to produce eight pieces of information in total. The number of details required is always made clear in each bullet point. Give what is required but don't add extra detail.

Education and work

Had a go ☐ Nearly there ☐ Nailed it! ☐

Applying for jobs

A job application

Listen to the recording

1 Marcos is talking about a job he has seen advertised. What does he say?

Write the correct letter in each box.

(a) The job is in a …

A	department store.
B	menswear shop.
C	shoe shop.

☐ **(1 mark)**

(b) They need someone to work …

A	full time.
B	afternoons only.
C	Saturdays.

☐ **(1 mark)**

(c) The advert specifies that …

A	sales experience is essential.
B	some experience is preferable.
C	no experience is necessary.

☐ **(1 mark)**

Dictation

Listen to the recording

2 You will hear four short sentences.

Listen carefully and using your knowledge of Spanish sounds, write down in **Spanish** exactly what you hear for each sentence. You will hear each sentence **three** times: the first time as a full sentence, the second time in short sections and the third time again as a full sentence.

Sentence 1

....

Sentence 2

....

Sentence 3

....

Sentence 4

....

(8 marks)

> Remember that two of the words will be taken from outside of the prescribed AQA vocabulary list. Don't worry about these, because they will obey the same spelling rules as all the words that you know and use regularly.

Had a go ☐ Nearly there ☐ Nailed it! ☐

Education and work

Preparing for interviews

Photo card

1 Talk about the content of these photos. You must say at least one thing about each photo.

(5 marks)

After you have spoken about the content of the photos, listen to the recording of further questions on the same topic. Pause the recording to give your answers. There is a sample recording in the Answers section to give you more ideas.

(20 marks)

> With the first picture, you will want to mention what the people are looking at. One man is looking at his watch (*el reloj*). In the second photo, you could describe what people are wearing and imagine how the young woman is feeling as well as describing what is happening.

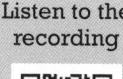

Translation

2 Translate these sentences into **English**.

Ayer fui a la oficina de turismo para una entrevista.

....

Llevé un traje gris, una camisa blanca y zapatos negros.

....

Me sentí bastante nervioso pero el jefe era simpático.

....

Hubo muchas preguntas, pero pude contestar con confianza.

....

Me dijo que me llamarían este jueves para decirme si he tenido éxito.

....

(10 marks)

> Be careful to translate verbs into the correct tense. Most of the verbs here relate to the past, but be careful with *llamarían*.

> Remember that the sentences in the exam won't all be on the same topic, but here you are practising the topic of **Education and work**.

Education and work

Had a go ☐ Nearly there ☐ Nailed it! ☐

Working to help others

Helping others

1 Emilio, Nadia and Malek are talking about what they do to help others. Answer the questions in **English**.

(a) How does Emilio help in the hospital?

.... (1 mark)

(b) What does Nadia do for her neighbour?

.... (1 mark)

(c) How does Malek help in the Home for the Elderly?

.... (1 mark)

> You cannot offer two answers. For example, if you are unsure what Nadia does because you can't decide whether she looks after her neighbour or does the neighbour's gardening, do not put down both – you will not be credited with a mark. You must choose between the two, and then at least you have a 50/50 chance of being right.

Picture task

2 You decide to send this photo on WhatsApp to a friend in Colombia.

What is in this photo? Write five short sentences in **Spanish**.

....

....

....

....

.... (10 marks)

Had a go ☐ Nearly there ☐ Nailed it! ☐

Free-time activities

Free-time activities

Dictation

1 You will hear four short sentences.

Listen carefully and using your knowledge of Spanish sounds, write down in **Spanish** exactly what you hear for each sentence. You will hear each sentence **three** times: the first time as a full sentence, the second time in short sections and the third time again as a full sentence.

Sentence 1

....

Sentence 2

....

Sentence 3

....

Sentence 4

....

(8 marks)

Reading aloud

2 Read aloud the text below in **Spanish**.

> Me interesa mucho el teatro.
> En el colegio me gusta participar en las obras que organizamos.
> Quisiera ser un actor famoso en el futuro.
> También me encanta jugar a los videojuegos.
> Hay algunos que son muy emocionantes.
> Con mi familia, me gusta descansar y ver películas graciosas en la televisión.

(5 marks)

Once you have read the text aloud, listen to the **four** recorded questions related to what you have read. Pause the recording after each one to give yourself time to answer.

In order to score the highest marks, you must try to answer all **four** questions as fully as you can.

(10 marks)

You can hear a recording of the text and sample answers from a student working at around Grade 9 in the Answers section.

35

Free-time activities

Had a go ☐ Nearly there ☐ Nailed it! ☐

Music and dance

Dance

1 You read this article about traditional dance in Spain.

> Mucha gente piensa que el flamenco es el baile tradicional de España pero, en realidad, es más típico del sur de España. Las varias regiones de España tienen sus propios bailes y están orgullosos de sus costumbres de música y baile. Por ejemplo, en la comunidad de Cataluña* el baile tradicional es la *Sardana*. Este baile se puede ver en las fiestas locales de los pueblos catalanes** o, durante los meses de verano, en la Plaza Sant Jaume I*** en Barcelona los domingos por la tarde. Otro baile tradicional del norte de España es la *Jota***** que se canta y se baila acompañada del sonido de las **castañuelas**. Se dice que este baile tiene sus orígenes en el siglo diecisiete.

Cataluña – Catalonia, a region in north-east Spain   **catalanes* – Catalan (from / in Catalonia)
****Plaza Sant Jaume I* – a square in Barcelona   *****la Jota* – a dance from the north of Spain

Complete these sentences. Write the letter for the correct option in each box.

(a) Flamenco …

A	is the Spanish national dance.
B	is a dance from the south of Spain.
C	is still danced by many people.

(b) The regions of Spain …

A	share the same customs.
B	all have hot weather.
C	are proud of their traditions.

(c) The *Sardana* is …

A	a regional dance.
B	traditional music.
C	a local festival.

(d) You can see the *Sardana* …

A	on some summer evenings.
B	most afternoons.
C	on Sunday mornings.

(e) Look at the second to last sentence again. What do you think *castañuelas* are?

A	costumes
B	musical instruments
C	dancers

(f) The dance called the *Jota* has its origins in …

A	the 16th century.
B	the 17th century.
C	the 18th century.

(6 marks)

An email about music

2 Write an email to your Chilean friend about music. Write approximately **50** words in **Spanish**. You must write something about each bullet point.

Mention:
- your favourite music
- a type of music you do not like
- when you listen to music
- if you play an instrument
- a concert you want to go to.

> You only have to write 10 words for each bullet to achieve the word count; it's not a huge amount, but you will have to extend each answer a little.

> Continue your answer on your own paper if you run out of space.

....
....
....

(10 marks)

Had a go ☐ Nearly there ☐ Nailed it! ☐

Free-time activities

Music and dance events

A TV dance show

1 Marcos and Andrea are talking about a TV dance show.

   What do they say?

   Write the correct letter in each box.

   (a) Andrea thought that …

A	the public got the vote right.
B	the couple did not deserve to be last.
C	the standard throughout was excellent.

   ☐ **(1 mark)**

   (b) Marcos …

A	agrees with Andrea.
B	thinks the opposite of Andrea.
C	is not sure what to think.

   ☐ **(1 mark)**

   (c) Marcos was not impressed by …

A	the woman with the short hair.
B	the model with the curly hair.
C	the actor with the blonde hair.

   ☐ **(1 mark)**

   (d) He believes the public vote for …

A	someone who is funny.
B	a pleasant personality.
C	the best dancer.

   ☐ **(1 mark)**

Translation

2 Translate these sentences into **English**.

   Tengo las entradas para el concierto.

   ....

   Creo que va a ser muy emocionante.

   ....

   Mi grupo favorito tocará sus últimas canciones.

   ....

   Ayer escuché su música y leí la letra.

   ....

   Vamos a pasarlo muy bien, estoy segura.

   ....

   (10 marks)

> The sentences in the exam will cover various topics but here you are practising the topic of **Free-time activities**.

Free-time activities

Had a go ☐ Nearly there ☐ Nailed it! ☐

Reading

Photo card

1 Talk about the content of these photos. You must say at least one thing about each photo.

(5 marks)

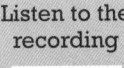

After you have spoken about the content of the photos, listen to the recording of further questions on the same topic. Pause the recording to give your answers. There is a sample recording in the Answers section to give you more ideas.

(20 marks)

> You may want to say the boy 'is surprised', or that the children 'are interested'. To do so, use *estar* for the verb 'to be', and *sorprendido* for 'surprised'. To say 'interested', use *interesado*. Both these words agree as they are being used as adjectives.

Translation

2 Translate the following sentences into **Spanish**.

I don't like to read newspapers.

....

This book has too many pages.

....

The main character is very nice.

....

My brother prefers science fiction novels.

....

Last week I read a story with a very sad ending.

....

(10 marks)

Had a go ☐ Nearly there ☐ Nailed it! ☐ **Free-time activities**

Television

An email about television

1 You are writing an email to your friend about television.

Write approximately **90** words in **Spanish**.

You must write something about each bullet point.

Mention:

- what sort of programmes you like to watch
- what you watched last week
- what you will watch this weekend.

....
....
....
....
....
....
....
....
....
....
....
....
....
....

(15 marks)

> Notice that the regular format of this type of question requires a present tense, a past tense and a future tense. If you know what to expect in the exam, you know how to focus your learning and your revision.

TV this evening

2 You hear a TV presenter announcing this evening's programmes.

What do they say? Write the correct letter in each box.

(a) Later on, you can see …

A	a political programme.
B	a drama series.
C	a song contest.

☐

(b) The next programme is for people interested in …

A	history.
B	nature.
C	sport.

☐

(2 marks)

Listen to the recording

> Listen carefully to the information about the programme that is on later. Take all the details into account and don't jump to conclusions on the strength of just one word.

Free-time activities

Had a go ☐ Nearly there ☐ Nailed it! ☐

The cinema

Reading aloud

1 Read aloud the following text in **Spanish**.

> Me gusta ir al cine, aunque cuesta mucho si compras bebidas y caramelos.
> Las entradas también son demasiado caras.
> Fui a ver una película extraña el jueves pasado.
> Al principio pensé que era divertida.
> Sin embargo, tenía un final tan triste que fue difícil no llorar.
> En general, prefiero las películas de miedo.

(5 marks)

Once you have read the text aloud, listen to the **four** recorded questions related to what you have read. Pause the recording after each one to give yourself time to answer.

In order to score the highest marks, you must try to answer all **four** questions as fully as you can.

(10 marks)

The letters 'j' and 'g' (when 'g' is followed by 'e' or 'i') are pronounced like the 'ch' in the Scottish word 'loch'. Listen to the recording of these words (*justo, tarjeta, colegio, página, coger, gente*) and practise saying them.

Other sounds tested in the passage include the following. Listen to the recording and practise saying the words:

('cu' + vowel) *cuenta, cuidar, cuatro*   ('ci') *cita, fácil, decir*   ('ll') *llegar, calle, ella*

Track 47

Translation

2 Translate the following sentences into **Spanish**.

My favourite film has some wonderful songs.

....

....

It is the story of a woman who wants to be a famous star.

....

....

It also won a lot of prizes.

....

Sometimes it is funny, but it has some sad moments at the end.

....

....

I am going to watch it again this weekend.

....

....

(10 marks)

> The translation on the Higher paper will contain an expression of past and future times as well as the present. There are 5 marks available for making the meaning clear and 5 marks for the accuracy of the vocabulary and grammar.

Had a go ☐   Nearly there ☐   Nailed it! ☐

Free-time activities

What's the story?

TV and film

1 Martín is talking about TV and film.

   Complete the sentences in **English**. Write **one** word in each space.

   (a) On TV, Martín likes to watch …………………………… films.   **(1 mark)**

   (b) In the cinema, he prefers …………………………… films.   **(1 mark)**

   (c) He goes to the cinema with his …………………………… .   **(1 mark)**

Photo card

2 Talk about the content of these photos. You must say at least one thing about each photo.

(5 marks)

After you have spoken about the content of the photos, listen to the recording of further questions on the same topic. Pause the recording to give your answers. There is a sample recording in the Answers section to give you more ideas.

(20 marks)

> Don't be afraid to take the initiative and steer the conversation towards an opportunity to show off what you know, as long as you have answered the question. Even if the question asks you what you do now, you could answer and then go on and say what you used to do or what you are going to do.

41

Customs, festivals and celebrations

Had a go ☐ Nearly there ☐ Nailed it! ☐

Everyday life

Family life

1 Miguel, Ana and David are talking about their daily routines. What do they say?

Write the correct letter in each box.

(a) During the week Miguel gets up at …

A	nine o'clock.
B	seven o'clock.
C	eight o'clock.

(1 mark)

(b) Ana says that, in her family, …

A	they often have a sleep in the day.
B	no one has time to have a sleep in the day.
C	only her grandmother has a sleep in the day.

(1 mark)

(c) David says …

A	he doesn't have breakfast.
B	he has a sandwich for breakfast.
C	he buys something to eat at school.

(1 mark)

> Remember that you have five minutes to read through the Listening paper questions before the recording starts. Always pay attention to the question titles, which tell you what topic each question is about. It's fine to make notes on the paper, as long as your answer to each question is clear and in the right place.

Translation

2 Translate the following sentences into **Spanish**.

I eat my breakfast in the kitchen.

....

Normally I get up at eight o'clock.

....

He leaves the house and catches the bus.

....

I do my homework after the evening meal.

....

Last weekend I watched television with my family.

....

(10 marks)

> Always have a go at as much of the translation as possible. If there are words you don't know, don't abandon the whole sentence, as you will get marks for all the sections that you can do.

Had a go ☐   Nearly there ☐   Nailed it! ☐

Customs, festivals and celebrations

Meals at home

Eating at home

1 You read Sara's blog about typical meals at home.

> Normalmente tomamos el desayuno a horas diferentes en mi casa porque todos tenemos un horario distinto. Yo no tomo mucho: algo de fruta y un café con mucha leche. Durante la semana comemos sobre las tres. Mi abuela prepara la comida porque mis padres trabajan. Sin embargo, todos volvemos a casa para comer y hablamos de nuestro día. A veces es un poco difícil porque mi hermana menor me molesta mucho cuando se niega a comer las verduras. La cena es una comida más ligera, y la tomamos sobre las nueve.

Answer the following questions in **English**.

(a) When do the family have breakfast?

....

(b) Who prepares lunch?

....

(c) What annoys Sara about her sister?

....

(d) How does Sara describe the evening meal?

....

(4 marks)

> It's very important to read carefully and not just assume the answer is the first relevant word you spot. There are three different people referred to in the text, so you have to find out which one of the three prepares the lunch to answer question (b).

Translation

2 Translate these sentences into **English**.

Tomo un bocadillo cuando vuelvo a casa.

....

Llevo fruta al colegio para comer durante el recreo.

....

Ayer cenamos a las diez.

....

Voy a servir el pollo con patatas fritas.

....

Me gusta ayudar a preparar la comida.

....

(10 marks)

> The translation in the exam will cover more than one topic, but here you are practising talking about food, for the topic **Healthy living and lifestyle**.

43

Customs, festivals and celebrations

Had a go ☐   Nearly there ☐   Nailed it! ☐

Celebrations

Listen to the recording

Dictation

1 You will hear four short sentences.

Listen carefully and, using your knowledge of Spanish sounds, write down in **Spanish** exactly what you hear for each sentence. You will hear each sentence **three** times: the first time as a full sentence, the second time in short sections and the third time again as a full sentence.

Sentence 1

....

....

Sentence 2

....

....

Sentence 3

....

....

Sentence 4

....

....

(8 marks)

> Remember that the letter 'h' is silent in Spanish. The verb *hacer*, in all tenses, begins with a silent 'h'. For example *hice* ('I did / made'), *haré* ('I will do / make') and *hago* ('I do / make'). Listen out for one of these in the dictation.

Picture task

2 You send this photo to your Peruvian friend.

What is in this photo?

Write **five** sentences in **Spanish**.

> It's a really good idea to study the present continuous tense so you can say what people **are doing** in the photo. It is not a difficult tense to learn: *estoy / estás / está / estamos / estáis / están* + *-ando* (for *-ar* verbs) or *-iendo* (for *-er* and *-ir* verbs). For example, *están celebrando* – 'they are celebrating'; *está abriendo* – 'he is opening'.

....

....

....

....

....

(10 marks)

Had a go ☐ Nearly there ☐ Nailed it! ☐

Customs, festivals and celebrations

Customs and festivals

St George's Day

1 You read this extract from a website about Barcelona.

> Según la tradición, el veintitrés de abril, o el Día de Sant Jordi, los hombres dan flores a sus novias y las mujeres responden regalando un libro a su novio. Cada año, las calles y las plazas de Barcelona se llenan de puestos de libros. Los vendedores* llegan temprano para montar los puestos y durante el día la gente visita los puestos para buscar el libro que quieren. A veces, hay un momento de emoción cuando el escritor o la escritora de un libro se presenta para firmar copias de su libro para las personas que los compran.
>
> La fiesta primero se celebró el 7 de octubre de 1926 pero luego la cambiaron al 23 de abril por ser el día en el que murieron dos de los escritores más famosos del mundo, el español Miguel de Cervantes (autor de *Don Quijote***) y el escritor inglés William Shakespeare.

vendedor – seller

**Don Quijote* – a novel written by the Spanish writer Cervantes in the 17th century

Answer the following questions in **English**.

(a) What **two** gifts are traditionally given on 23rd April?

.... **(2 marks)**

(b) What happens to the streets and squares of Barcelona on that day?

.... **(1 mark)**

(c) What happens early on the day?

.... **(1 mark)**

(d) What exciting event sometimes happens?

.... **(1 mark)**

(e) What is significant about 7th October 1926?

.... **(1 mark)**

(f) Why was the event moved?

.... **(1 mark)**

> If there is a word in a reading text that is not on the AQA vocabulary list and which is not easy to work out (like *vendedor* – 'seller') then it will be 'glossed'. That means the word will have an asterisk (*) and the meaning will be given underneath the text.

The April Fair

2 Sofía is talking about her visit to the April Fair in Seville, a city in the south of Spain.

What aspects does she mention? Choose the **three** correct statements.

Write the correct letters in the boxes.

A	costumes	D	horse parade
B	dancing	E	singing
C	food	F	weather

☐ ☐ ☐

(3 marks)

Customs, festivals and celebrations

Had a go ☐   Nearly there ☐   Nailed it! ☐

Spanish festivals

The *Tomatina* festival

1. You are listening to a radio phone-in. Four people give their opinions on the *Tomatina* festival.

   What opinion does each one express?

   Write **P** for a positive opinion

   N for a negative opinion

   P+N for a positive and negative opinion.

   Write the correct letter in each box.

   (a) Speaker 1 ☐

   (b) Speaker 2 ☐

   (c) Speaker 3 ☐

   (d) Speaker 4 ☐   **(4 marks)**

   > With this type of question, make sure your answer is totally clear. If you change your mind, cross out the incorrect answer very clearly and write your new answer next to the box. If an examiner can see more than one answer, and neither is crossed out, you cannot be awarded a mark.

A village festival

2. You read a leaflet about events at a local village festival.

   > Enhorabuena a los estudiantes de la escuela de baile por el concierto de anoche. Fue un gran éxito. Hoy te invitamos a probar comida y bebidas típicas de la región en los puestos de la plaza mayor. Recordaréis que el año pasado organizamos paseos a caballo en el parque, pero no ha sido posible ofrecer esta oportunidad este año. Sin embargo, mañana en la playa hay un concurso de castillos de arena para los niños. Habrá premios para los ganadores.

   What does it say about these events?

   Write **P** for something that happened **in the past**

   N for something that is happening **now**

   F for something that is going to happen **in the future**.

   Write the correct letter in each box.

   (a) Dance show ☐

   (b) Food and drink sampling ☐

   (c) Horse rides in the park ☐

   (d) Sandcastle competition ☐   **(4 marks)**

   > In these questions you are looking for two types of clues. Firstly, look for the tenses of the verbs that will tell you whether something happens in the past, present or future. Also, look for time phrases like *anoche* ('last night'), *ahora* ('now') and *mañana* ('tomorrow').

Had a go ☐ Nearly there ☐ Nailed it! ☐   **Customs, festivals and celebrations**

Latin American festivals

A fifteenth birthday

1 You read this article about a Mexican tradition.

> En México, cuando una chica llega a los quince años, muchas familias celebran la ocasión con una gran celebración. Tradicionalmente es la edad cuando una chica deja de ser una niña y se convierte en una mujer. Para la fiesta, la chica se viste con un vestido largo y baila el primer baile con su padre. Como regalo, le dan una última muñeca* – lo que significa que ya no es una niña. Durante la fiesta la chica se cambia los zapatos por unos de tacón** alto, que representan que ya es adulta.

muñeca – doll   **tacón* – heel

Answer the following questions in **English**.

(a) Traditionally, what is significant about a girl's fifteenth birthday?

....

(b) What does the girl wear for her party?

....

(c) What does the article tell us about the dancing at the party?

....

(d) What is the significance of the gift she is given?

....

(e) What symbolic act does the girl do during the party?

.... **(5 marks)**

> Remember that in the Reading exam, you may meet words that are not on the prescribed vocabulary list. Their meaning will usually be very obvious, like *adulta* ('adult'). If not, they will be glossed (explained via an asterisk) like *muñeca* and *tacón* above.

Photo card

2 Talk about the content of these photos. You must say at least one thing about each photo.

(5 marks)

After you have spoken about the content of the photos, listen to the recording of further questions on the same topic. Pause the recording to give your answers. There is a sample recording in the Answers section to give you more ideas. **(20 marks)**

> Remember to look at the background of the photos as well, to give you more ideas of things to say. The phrase *Al fondo* (Higher) can introduce your description; it means 'in the background'.

Celebrity culture   Had a go ☐   Nearly there ☐   Nailed it! ☐

My favourite celebrity

A Spanish singer

1. You read this article about the singer Amaia.

> La cantante Amaia tiene veinticinco años y es de Pamplona, en el norte de España. De joven participó en muchos concursos de talento y, en 2018, ganó el famoso concurso de televisión *Operación Triunfo**. Desde entonces, ha representado a su país en el *Festival de la canción de Eurovisión* y ha grabado dos álbumes de estudio. No solo canta. También es una pianista excelente y escribe sus propias canciones. El año pasado hizo su primer papel como actriz en una serie de televisión.

*Operación Triunfo – a TV reality music show

What does the article tell us?

Write   **A** if only statement **A** is correct

         B if only statement **B** is correct

         A+B if both statements **A** and **B** are correct.

Write the correct letter in each box.

> Remember that the questions come in the same order as the text.

(a) Amaia …

A	is in her mid-twenties.
B	is from northern Spain.

(c) Amaia …

A	won the Eurovision Song Contest.
B	has recorded two studio albums.

(b) Amaia …

A	took part in talent shows.
B	came second in *Operación Triunfo*.

(d) Amaia …

A	is a singer-songwriter.
B	has had acting roles.

(4 marks)

My favourite singer

2. You are writing an article about music.

Write approximately **90** words in **Spanish**.

You must write something about each bullet point.

Mention:
- your favourite group or singer
- what the group / singer has done in the past
- when you will next listen to their music.

> The bullet points are deliberately left quite open to allow you plenty of options of what to write about. For example, for bullet point 2, you could talk about childhood, origins, awards, concerts, best songs, etc.

....
....
....
....
....
....
....

(15 marks)

Had a go ☐ **Nearly there** ☐ **Nailed it!** ☐ | Celebrity culture

Profile of a celebrity

Role play

1 You are talking to your Spanish friend.

Listen to the recording of the teacher's part. The teacher will play the part of your friend and will speak first.

You should address your friend as *tú*.

When you see this – ? – you will have to ask a question.

> 1 Say who your favourite famous person is.
> 2 Say what the person does.
> 3 Say what the person looks like.
> 4 Say where you watch this person.
> ?5 Ask your friend about television in Spain.

(10 marks)

> In order to score full marks, you must include a verb in your response to each task.

> The role plays aim to be as open as possible so you can choose from a range of options to talk about. Here, the famous person could be a singer, musician, sportsperson, presenter, actor etc.

TV personalities

2 Write an email to your Chilean friend about famous people on TV.

Write approximately **50** words in **Spanish**.

You must write something about each bullet point.

Mention:

- your favourite TV programme
- what the programme is about
- when it is on
- someone who is in the programme
- what you think of this person.

> The tasks are designed to avoid the opportunity for repetition. However, to be on the safe side, make sure that you don't repeat yourself by using the same information for more than one of the bullet points.

....
....
....
....
....
....

(10 marks)

49

Celebrity culture Had a go ☐ Nearly there ☐ Nailed it! ☐

Celebrities as role models

Celebrities

1 You read this article from an online magazine.

> **Hugo González** es un cantante cubano que es muy popular en las redes sociales, no solo por su música. Sus seguidores lo respetan por lo que hace para ayudar a la gente que vive en la calle.
>
> **Alba Castro**, la actriz colombiana, salió en una revista la semana pasada porque ha creado una campaña para apoyar a las víctimas de violencia. La actriz es un buen modelo a seguir.
>
> **Emilio Morales,** el jugador de fútbol boliviano, dedica unas horas cada semana para trabajar en un banco de comida cerca de su casa. Insiste en que es lo menos que puede hacer.

Which comment matches which person?

Write **H** for **Hugo**

A for **Alba**

E for **Emilio.**

Write the correct letter in each box.

Who …

(a)	… is Colombian?	
(b)	… helps in a food bank?	
(c)	… is Cuban?	
(d)	… helps victims of violence?	
(e)	… is Bolivian?	
(f)	… helps the homeless?	

> It is a good idea to read through the question first so that you know what information you are looking for when you read the text. Then read the text all the way through before you start putting your answers in the grid. As you read, you could highlight the essential sections in the text where you have found key information for the answers.

(6 marks)

2 **Translation**

Translate the following sentences into **Spanish**.

They published a photo of the singer's girlfriend in a magazine.

....

....

The player's behaviour has had an impact on the club's image.

....

....

I respect the musician because he is a good role model.

....

....

She is going to use her money to help other people.

....

The band sets a good example to young people.

....

(10 marks)

Had a go ☐ Nearly there ☐ Nailed it! ☐   **Celebrity culture**

TV reality shows

Reading aloud

1 Read aloud the following text in **Spanish**.

> Algunas personas que participan en los concursos solo quieren ser ricas y famosas.
>
> Otras son músicos y buscan una carrera como cantantes porque tienen buena voz.
>
> Muchos vuelven a su antiguo trabajo después de un año.

(5 marks)

Now play the recording to listen to and answer **four** questions that relate to the topic of **Celebrity culture**. In order to score the highest marks, you must try to answer all **four** questions as fully as you can.

(10 marks)

> Be careful with the word *músicos*. When we say 'music' in English, the sound is like this 'mew - zik'. In Spanish, the 'u' is more like 'oo' and the 's' is a real 's' sound and not a 'z'.
>
> Listen to these words and practise them out loud:
>
> *música, museo, usar*

Track 57

Magazine headlines

2 You see some headlines in a Spanish online magazine.

A	Programa cancelado por huelgas en el estudio
B	Se divorcian dos estrellas de *La isla del amor*
C	Lucía dice que se ha enamorado de su pareja de baile
D	Una abuela de setenta y ocho años gana programa de cocina
E	Más de nueve millones vieron el último episodio de la serie

Which headline matches each description? Write the correct letter in each box.

(a) The relationship did not last   ☐

(b) Huge audiences for the final show   ☐

(c) The partners could become a couple   ☐

(3 marks)

Celebrity culture   Had a go ☐   Nearly there ☐   Nailed it! ☐

The good and the bad of being famous

Photo card

1. Talk about the content of these photos. You must say at least one thing about each photo. **(5 marks)**

After you have spoken about the content of the photos, listen to the recording of further questions on the topic of **Celebrity culture.** Pause the recording to give your answers. There is a sample recording in the Answer section to give you more ideas. **(20 marks)**

> During your preparation time, look at the two photos and make as many notes as you wish on paper. You can use these notes during the test. When talking about the content of these photos, keep in mind that the recommended time is approximately one minute at Foundation tier.

A talent show

2. On Spanish TV, you listen to a talent show winner talking about her experiences.

   What is her opinion of these aspects?

   Write   **P** for a **positive** opinion

           N for a **negative** opinion

           P+N for a **positive** and **negative** opinion.

   (a) Recording in the studio   ☐

   (b) Being recognised in the street   ☐

   (c) Relationship with the record company   ☐

   (d) The sales of her music   ☐

   (4 marks)

Had a go ☐ Nearly there ☐ Nailed it! ☐

Travel and tourism

Plans for the holidays

Holiday plans

1 Marta is talking about her holiday plans.

Write the correct letters in the boxes.

| A | Eating out | C | Going to the coast | E | Reading | G | Sunbathing |
| B | Gardening | D | Having a lie-in | F | Serving customers | H | Working |

What **two** activities is she planning to do …

(a) on the first day? ☐ ☐ **(2 marks)**

(b) at weekends? ☐ ☐ **(2 marks)**

(c) in August? ☐ ☐ **(2 marks)**

> Always listen out for key words that link to the questions – these will alert you to the fact that you are about to hear an answer. You could highlight key words in the exam in the preparation time at the start. Here, key words are: 'first, weekends, August'.

Making plans

2 You read Luis and Hugo's texts about holiday plans.

> **Luis:** ¿Vamos a la piscina mañana?
>
> **Hugo:** Pero mañana es sábado, habrá demasiada gente. ¿El lunes?
>
> **Luis:** Los lunes está cerrada para limpiar. ¿Qué te parece si montamos en bicicleta mañana y vamos a la piscina el martes?
>
> **Hugo:** Perfecto. Llevaré bocadillos y una bebida para tomar durante la excursión.

Answer the questions in **English.**

(a) Where does Luis first suggest they go?

....

(b) Why does Hugo think it's a bad idea?

....

(c) What day does Hugo suggest?

....

(d) What is the problem with Hugo's suggestion?

....

(e) What is Luis's new idea for tomorrow?

....

(f) What will Hugo bring?

.... **(6 marks)**

Travel and tourism

Had a go ☐ Nearly there ☐ Nailed it! ☐

Holiday preferences

Holiday destinations

1 Read these social media comments about the ideal holiday destination.

> **Lola:** Me gustaría pasar un rato con mis primos ingleses. Necesito practicar el idioma y Londres es el sitio ideal para visitar edificios históricos.
>
> **David:** Siempre quiero ir a montañas en verano, por el aire fresco. Quedarse en la ciudad o en la costa es muy difícil en agosto porque hace mucho calor.
>
> **Alba:** Yo preferiría ir a la costa del sur. Hay mucho que hacer para los jóvenes y el viaje para llegar allí es muy corto.

Where would Lola, David and Alba like to go and why?

	Destination
A	Abroad
B	Coast
C	City
D	Countryside
E	Mountains

	Reason
1	The beaches
2	The culture
3	It's cooler
4	Short journey
5	The warm weather

Write the correct **letter** for the destination. Write the correct **number** for the reason.

	Destination	Reason	
(a) Lola	☐	☐	(2 marks)
(b) David	☐	☐	(2 marks)
(c) Alba	☐	☐	(2 marks)

> Take care to look closely at all the instructions for a question. When a question requires more than one answer, sometimes it doesn't matter which order you put them in. Here, you need to ensure you put letters in the first box, for the destinations, and numbers in the second box, for the reasons.

General conversation

2 After the Photo card in the exam, you won't see the general conversation questions written down, you will only hear your teacher asking them.

Play the recording to hear some questions on the topic of **Holiday preferences**. If necessary, pause the recording after each question and think about how to answer it, before giving your answer.

(10 marks)

> If you give a short opinion without a reason, your teacher may ask ¿Por qué?' to encourage you to explain your reason. However, the mark scheme credits you for giving extended sequences of speech so it is better for you to show you can develop your replies with reasons and explanations.

Had a go ☐ Nearly there ☐ Nailed it! ☐

Travel and tourism

Types of holidays

Holiday preferences

1 Read the comments from an internet forum.

> **Fátima:** A mí me gusta más ir en coche para visitar las ciudades y los pueblos históricos de mi región. Me encanta visitar los edificios y monumentos construidos hace muchos años.
>
> **Luis:** Yo siempre busco vacaciones activas, pero en el campo. Por ejemplo, me gusta montar a caballo y nadar en los ríos.
>
> **Pilar:** En general prefiero pasar tiempo en la ciudad porque me gusta ver las tiendas, comprar ropa y recuerdos y comer en restaurantes buenos.

Match the correct person with each of the following questions.

Write **F** for Fátima

L for Luis

P for Pilar.

Write the correct letter in each box.

Who likes to …

(a)	… go shopping?	
(b)	… be in the countryside?	
(c)	… travel around?	
(d)	… eat out?	
(e)	… go sightseeing?	
(f)	… get some exercise?	

(6 marks)

> With this type of comprehension task, the questions (a)–(f) do not come in the same order as the text. This means you need to look at the questions in turn, then scan the texts to find a relevant word. Start with 'go shopping' from question (a), then skim-read through the comments until you find a word that suggests shopping, then read it in detail to make sure you have found the real answer.

Photo card

2 Talk about the content of these photos. You must say at least **one** thing about each photo.

(5 marks)

After you have spoken about the content of the photos, listen to the recording of further questions on the same topic. Pause the recording to give your answers. There is a sample recording in the Answers section to give you more ideas.

(20 marks)

> Don't worry if there are things in the first photo that you do not know the words for.
>
> If you don't know 'tent' – *hacen camping* ('they are camping')
>
> If you don't know 'wood / forest' – *están en el campo* ('they are in the countryside'), *hay muchos árboles* ('there are lots of trees')

> You can listen to a sample answer from a student working at around Grade 8 in the Answers section.

Travel and tourism

Had a go ☐ Nearly there ☐ Nailed it! ☐

Where to stay

Where to stay on holiday

1 Elena, Javier and Indra are talking about where they prefer to stay on holiday.
   What do they say? Write the correct letter in each box.

(a) Elena and her family prefer an apartment because …

A	it's more private.
B	it's cheaper than a hotel.
C	it gives them more room.

(b) Elena says that having an apartment means …

A	you can cook when you want.
B	you can eat in different places.
C	you have more freedom.

(c) Javier's family think that being in a five-star hotel means you get …

A	bigger rooms.
B	excellent waiters.
C	better food.

(d) In a five-star hotel, there is …

A	a wide range of facilities.
B	room service.
C	24-hour reception.

(e) Indra's idea of a perfect holiday is …

A	on a campsite with facilities.
B	camping in the woods.
C	in a house in the country.

(f) Indra wants …

A	to be close to restaurants and a pool.
B	to have modern washing facilities.
C	to get back to nature.

(6 marks)

> This is a multiple-choice style question and you will see these a lot on the Listening exam on both the Foundation and Higher papers. All the options will be plausible, so you need to listen carefully so you eliminate the wrong answers and select the correct one. If you really don't know the answer, guess! You have a 33% chance of getting it right, whereas a blank box is definitely wrong.

Translation

2 Translate the following sentences into **Spanish**.

The facilities in the hotel are excellent.

....

We are going to stay in a three-star campsite.

....

I hope to rent a house close to the beach.

....

The apartment was very clean, and it had a view of the pool.

....

It rained on Thursday when we went to the theme park.

....

(10 marks)

Had a go ☐ Nearly there ☐ Nailed it! ☐   **Travel and tourism**

Booking accommodation

Listen to the recording

Booking a room

1 You are at the reception desk in a hotel and hear a woman booking a room.

   What **three** things does she mention?

   Write the correct letters in the boxes.

A	A map of the area	D	Restaurant opening times
B	Booking a table	E	Type of view
C	Number of nights	F	Where the stairs are

☐ ☐ ☐

(3 marks)

> These are called 'selection' questions because you just select the correct options from a list. There are always double the number of options than answers required. So, here, for three answers, you have six possible options.

Listen to the recording

Dictation

2 You will hear four short sentences.

   Listen carefully and using your knowledge of Spanish sounds, write down in **Spanish** exactly what you hear for each sentence. You will hear each sentence **three** times: the first time as a full sentence, the second time in short sections and the third time again as a full sentence.

Sentence 1

....

....

Sentence 2

....

....

Sentence 3

....

....

Sentence 4

....

....

(8 marks)

> Remember that when you hear a sound like the 'ni' in 'o**ni**on', this is the letter *ñ* in Spanish. You have come across it lots of times in words like *España* and *español*.

Travel and tourism

Had a go ☐ Nearly there ☐ Nailed it! ☐

Holiday activities

Picture task

1 You decide to send this photo on WhatsApp to a Spanish friend.

> If at first glance you think there isn't enough to say, keep looking. You can mention: how many people there are, where they are, what they are doing and what the weather is like.

What is in this photo?

Write **five** sentences in **Spanish**.

....

....

....

....

.... **(10 marks)**

Reading aloud

2 Read aloud the following text in **Spanish**.

> Ayer dimos un paseo en bicicleta.
> Hoy vamos a montar a caballo.
> Quiero hacer una excursión en barco mañana.
> Después voy a jugar al baloncesto.
> Hace cuatro días fuimos al parque.
> El perro estaba contento allí.

> You can check your reading by listening to a recording of the text in the Answers section. You can also hear sample answers to the questions.

(5 marks)

Once you have read the text aloud, listen to the **four** recorded questions related to what you have read. Pause the recording after each one to give yourself time to answer.

In order to score the highest marks, you must try to answer all **four** questions as fully as you can.

(10 marks)

> Remember that in the combinations of letters *que* and *qui* the 'u' sound is not pronounced, so you get 'keh' and 'ki' (not 'kweh' and 'kwi').
>
> It is when 'c' is followed by 'u' that the 'u' sound **does** get pronounced (as in *cuatro, escuela* and *cuidar*).
>
> Listen to these words to practise them:
>
> *que, queremos, pequeño*
>
> *quitar, tranquilo, equipo*
>
> *cuatro, escuela, cuidar*

Track 67

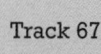

Had a go ☐ Nearly there ☐ Nailed it! ☐   **Travel and tourism**

Trips and visits

Role play

Listen to the recording

1 You are talking to the receptionist in a hotel.

Listen to the recording of the teacher's part. The teacher will play the part of the receptionist and will speak first.

You should address the receptionist as *tú*.

When you see this – **?** – you will have to ask a question.

> 1 Say when you would like to go on a trip. (Give **two** details.)
> 2 Say what time you want to go. (Give **one** detail.)
> 3 Say what sort of trip you would like. (Give **one** detail and **one** reason)
> ?4 Ask about the price of the tickets.
> 5 Give your opinion of the hotel. (Give **one** opinion and **one** reason.)

In the exam, the role play will be an informal conversation with, for example, a friend.

In order to score full marks, you must include a verb in your response to each task.

(10 marks)

> You can't know exactly what the teacher's role is going to be so you cannot be sure exactly how the questions or comments by the teacher will be phrased. For this reason, you should prepare a full phrase or sentence to each bullet point. So for the first bullet point, don't just say *Jueves* ('Thursday'). You need to say, in Spanish, 'I prefer to go on Thursday' or 'I want to go on Thursday'.

Translation

2 Translate these sentences into **English**.

Hace varios días, hicimos una excursión a las montañas al norte de la ciudad.

....
....

Fuimos en autobús y el viaje duró una hora y media.

....
....

Nos paramos en un pueblo para comer y había flores por todas partes.

....
....

Hoy estamos comprando recuerdos en el mercado.

....
....

Tengo muchas ganas de visitar el castillo mañana.

....
....

(10 marks)

> Avoid gaps if at all possible. For instance, if you don't know *nos paramos*, but you know everything else that is around the verb, then give a translation that makes sense instead of leaving a gap. Educated guesswork is a very useful skill!

59

Travel and tourism

Had a go ☐ Nearly there ☐ Nailed it! ☐

Giving and asking for directions

Role play

1 You are asking a friend for help in town.

Listen to the recording of the teacher's part. The teacher will play the part of your friend and will speak first.

You should address your friend as *tú*.

When you see this –?– you will have to ask a question.

> ?1 Ask a question about the shop opening times.
> 2 Say what you want to buy.
> 3 Say what you think of the town. (Give **one** detail.)
> 4 Say where you are staying. (Give **one** detail.)
> 5 Say when you are returning home.

> In order to score full marks, you must include a verb in your response to each task.

(10 marks)

> If you forget how to say 'to stay', you can get round it by saying, in Spanish, 'We are in the hotel + name' (*Estamos en el Hotel ....*) or 'we have a house / flat near the beach' (*Tenemos una casa / un piso cerca de la playa*).

Getting instructions

2 You read Mario's instructions on how to get to the café to meet him.

> Sal de casa y sigue la calle a la derecha. Al final, pasa por el puente. Después, continúa hasta la biblioteca y toma la calle a la izquierda. A unos cincuenta metros, al lado del parque, está el Café Carmen. Te veo allí a las siete.

Answer the following questions in **English**.

(a) What should you do on leaving the house?

....

(b) What must you do at the end of the street?

....

(c) What do you do when you reach the library?

....

(d) How far along the street is the café?

....

(e) What is next to the café?

....

(f) What time will he be there?

....

(6 marks)

Had a go ☐ Nearly there ☐ Nailed it! ☐   **Travel and tourism**

Tourist information

Dictation

1 You will hear five short sentences.

Listen carefully and using your knowledge of Spanish sounds, write down in **Spanish** exactly what you hear for each sentence. You will hear each sentence **three** times: the first time as a full sentence, the second time in short sections and the third time again as a full sentence.

Sentence 1

....
....

Sentence 2

....
....

Sentence 3

....
....

Sentence 4

....
....

Sentence 5

....
....

(10 marks)

> Use your understanding of the language to help you separate words. When we speak, we naturally run words into each other, especially when one word ends with a vowel and the next word begins with a vowel. So if you hear what sounds like *vana*, it is probably a vowel.

Translation

2 Translate the following sentences into **Spanish**.

I am going to the tourist office.

....

We want a list of hotels in the area.

....

The map shows many interesting places.

....

I asked for information about the festival.

....

The castle is not open to the public.

....

(10 marks)

Travel and tourism

Had a go ☐ Nearly there ☐ Nailed it! ☐

Tourist attractions

Translation

1 Translate these sentences into **English**.

Acabamos de pasar el día en Barcelona.

....

Sin duda, es una ciudad hermosa con muchos sitios de interés.

....

Disfruté pasear por la calle desde la plaza hasta el puerto, con todos los puestos de flores.

....

Vale la pena ir a ver el parque y los edificios.

....

La arquitectura es muy interesante.

....

(10 marks)

> There will be some challenging parts of the translation at Higher tier but there will also be some more straightforward parts. The translation, like all parts of the Higher paper, is designed to test ability ranges from Grade 4 up to Grade 9. So don't panic at the trickier bits, and attempt as much as you can.

Places to visit

2 You are writing an email to your Spanish friend about the local tourist attractions.

Write approximately **90** words in **Spanish**.

You must write something about each bullet point.

Mention:

- what there is to see in your area
- what you did in the city last week
- an activity that your friend can do when he visits.

> For the last bullet point you could suggest an activity you and your friend could do together:
>
> *Durante tu visita, ¿por qué no vamos a …?*
> 'During your visit, why don't we go to …?'
>
> OR
>
> *Durante tu visita, hay un concierto / una fiesta. ¿Quieres ir?*
> 'During your visit, there is a concert / a party. Do you want to go?'

....

....

....

....

....

....

....

....

....

(15 marks)

Had a go ☐ Nearly there ☐ Nailed it! ☐

Travel and tourism

Holiday problems

Hotel reviews

1 Read these reviews by customers of a hotel.

> No estaba contenta con el hotel y no volvería. Varias veces, cuando comimos en el restaurante, la comida estaba fría. *Martina*
>
> Cuando llegué, vi que el baño de la habitación estaba sucio. Lo limpiaron después, pero no me dio una buena imagen del hotel. *Nicolás*
>
> La luz al lado de la cama no funcionaba. Hablamos con el hombre en la recepción sobre el problema, pero no hizo nada mientras estuvimos allí. *Lucía*

What problem does each one complain about?

Write the correct letter in each box.

A	bed not comfortable
B	broken window
C	cold food
D	dirty bathroom
E	light not working
F	staff not being pleasant

Don't just rely on the information from one word. You might see the verb *limpiar* and recognise that it means 'to clean'. This could mislead you. When you read around you will find that they had to clean the room because it was dirty.

(a) Martina ☐

(b) Nicolás ☐

(c) Lucía ☐

(3 marks)

Holiday website

2 You are writing a post for a Spanish website about holidays.

Write approximately **150** words in **Spanish**.

You must write something about both bullet points. Mention:

- what sort of holidays you like
- where you would like to visit in the future.

For the second writing task on the Higher paper, you are recommended to write approximately 150 words. There is a choice of two options for the question so there will be two different topics to choose from.

Continue your answer on your own paper if you run out of space here.

....

....

....

....

....

....

....

....

(25 marks)

Travel and tourism

Had a go ☐ Nearly there ☐ Nailed it! ☐

Accommodation problems

A camping trip

1. Nicolás is speaking to the campsite receptionist.

   Answer the questions in **English**.

   (a) Who is Nicolás camping with?

   ....

   (b) Whereabouts on the site are they camping?

   ....

   (c) Why are they having trouble sleeping?

   ....

   (d) What rule are some young people breaking?

   ....

   (e) What is Nicolás' first idea for a solution?

   ....

   (f) What is his preferred solution?

   ....

   (6 marks)

> Always read the questions carefully before the recording begins. It can help to highlight key words in the questions, and this ensures you do read them properly instead of skim-reading.

Translation

2. Translate the following sentences into **Spanish**.

   There is a problem with the bill.

   ....

   The windows in the apartment are dirty.

   ....

   The hotel does not have a restaurant.

   ....

   We asked for a room with a view of the sea.

   ....

   I am not happy with the bed.

   ....

   (10 marks)

> Remember that *pedir* means 'to ask **for**', so you don't need an extra word to translate 'for'.
>
> Don't forget to make adjectives agree: for example, 'dirty' needs to agree with the noun it describes.

Had a go ☐   **Nearly there** ☐   **Nailed it!** ☐

Travel and tourism

Eating out

Role play

1 You are talking to your Spanish friend.

Listen to the recording of the teacher's part. The teacher will play the part of your friend and will speak first.

You should address your friend as *tú*.

When you see this – **?** – you will have to ask a question.

> 1 Say what your favourite food is. (Give **one** detail.)
> 2 Say where you go to eat out. (Give **one** detail.)
> 3 Say who you go with.
> ?4 Ask your friend a question about a restaurant.
> 5 Say what you think about Spanish food. (Give **one** detail.)

(10 marks)

> In order to score full marks, you must include a verb in your response to each task.

> Remember that it is perfectly all right to use vocabulary that is not on the AQA vocabulary list in the speaking and writing tasks. So if you know words for food and drink that are not on the list, you can certainly use them, as long as they are correct.

In a restaurant

2 Julia is talking to a waiter in the restaurant. Answer the questions in **English**.

(a) What does Julia first ask for?

....

(b) Where is her table?

....

(c) What does Julia want to know?

....

(d) What does the waiter tell her?

....

(e) What does her friend want to eat?

....

(f) What do they order to drink?

....

(6 marks)

Travel and tourism

Had a go ☐   Nearly there ☐   Nailed it! ☐

Opinions about food

Photo card

1 Talk about the content of these photos. You must say at least one thing about each photo.

(5 marks)

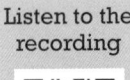

After you have spoken about the content of the photos, listen to the recording of further questions on the same topic. Pause the recording to give your answers. There is a sample recording in the Answers section to give you more ideas.

(20 marks)

> During the preparation time, make sure you jot down ideas in Spanish about both photos. If you find yourself saying a lot about one photo and not much about the other, that's fine, as long as both are mentioned.

Dictation

2 You will hear four short sentences. Listen carefully and using your knowledge of Spanish sounds, write down in **Spanish** exactly what you hear for each sentence. You will hear each sentence **three** times: the first time as a full sentence, the second time in short sections and the third time again as a full sentence.

Sentence 1

....

Sentence 2

....

Sentence 3

....

Sentence 4

....

(8 marks)

> When two vowels come together, you will hear each one.
> In *paella*, both the 'a' and 'e' sounds are heard, in *demasiado* you can hear the 'i' and the 'a'. In *prefiero* you will hear the 'i' and the 'e'.

Had a go ☐   Nearly there ☐   Nailed it! ☐

Travel and tourism

The weather

Picture task

1 You decide to send this photo on WhatsApp to a friend in Argentina.

What is in this photo? Write **five** sentences in **Spanish**.

....

....

....

....

....

(10 marks)

> You may not know all the words for the things you see (like 'umbrella', for instance) but don't try to invent something that you don't know. Look at the rest of the photo and focus on the things that you do know. Words that are on the prescribed AQA vocabulary list include 'bench' (*el banco*), 'tree' (*el árbol*), 'river' (*el río*) and 'to rain' (*llover*).

Translation

2 Translate these sentences into **English**.

Hace mucho frío hoy.

....

Vamos a tener temperaturas muy altas esta tarde.

....

Mañana hará calor y sol todo el día.

....

Hizo viento en la costa ayer.

....

Está lloviendo y hay muchas nubes grises en el cielo.

....

(10 marks)

> Be careful of the tenses in these sentences. There are verbs in the present (Sentence 1 and 5), the future (Sentence 3), the immediate future (Sentence 2) and the preterite (Sentence 4).

Media and technology

Had a go ☐ Nearly there ☐ Nailed it! ☐

Me and my mobile

Picture task

1 You decide to send this photo to a friend in Mexico.

What is in this photo? Write **five** sentences in **Spanish**.

....

....

....

....

.... **(10 marks)**

> You only need the present tense in this question on the Foundation writing paper but, if verbs are not your strong point, learn *hay* ('there is / there are'), *tiene* ('he / she has'), *tienen* ('they have'), *está en* ('he / she is in') and *están en* ('they are in').
>
> These will allow you to say a variety of things.

Dictation

2 You will hear four short sentences. Listen carefully and using your knowledge of Spanish sounds, write down in **Spanish** exactly what you hear for each sentence. You will hear each sentence **three** times: the first time as a full sentence, the second time in short sections and the third time again as a full sentence.

Listen to the recording

Sentence 1

....

....

Sentence 2

....

....

Sentence 3

....

....

Sentence 4

....

....

(8 marks)

Had a go ☐ **Nearly there** ☐ **Nailed it!** ☐

Media and technology

Social media

Target grade 6

Networking

1 Marco, Amira, Javier and Sofía are talking about social networks.

What aspect does each one mention?

Write the correct letter in each box.

A	business advertising
B	finding romance
C	following celebrities
D	hurtful comments
E	online entertainment
F	sharing your hobbies

(a) Marco ☐

(b) Amira ☐

(c) Javier ☐

(c) Sofía ☐

(4 marks)

> Often, you won't hear the exact words from the grid in the recordings. The options in the grid tend to be a summary of the comments made. The recording uses other words that lead you to the phrase used in the answer options.

Target grade 1-5

Reading aloud

2 Read aloud the following text in **Spanish**.

> Es muy importante no subir información peligrosa a tu página.
> Dicen que algunos jefes miran las redes sociales.
> La gente puede perder su trabajo.
> Recomiendan no compartir demasiados detalles.
> Si lo haces, alguien podría robarlos.

(5 marks)

> You can make notes on paper when you prepare for the Read aloud task. Try to work out the meaning of the text during the preparation time, and jot down any words after which you think there is a slight natural pause in the sentence. For instance, in the fourth sentence, you could note down the word *detalles*. The sentence means 'They recommend not to share too many details' and the last one means 'if you do, someone could steal them'. By recognising the meaning of the passage, the way you read it will make it clear that you do understand what you are saying.

> To check your pronunciation, you can hear a recording of the text in the Answers section.

Media and technology — Had a go ☐ Nearly there ☐ Nailed it! ☐

The internet

The internet

1 You hear David, Ana and Miguel talking about the internet. What do they say?
   Write the correct letter in each box.

   (a) David thinks that …

A	the internet is brilliant for studying.
B	the information is not always accurate.
C	people are not who they say they are.

   ☐

   (b) Ana says that …

A	the internet is really fast in her house.
B	there is too much information out there.
C	it's not hard to work out what is true.

   ☐

   (c) Miguel says that using the internet means that …

A	homework takes him even longer.
B	he spends too much time playing games online.
C	he saves time doing his school work.

   ☐

   (3 marks)

My mother's hobby

2 You read Sara's article about her mother's hobby.

> A mi madre le encanta viajar e ir de vacaciones. Le gusta hacer durar la experiencia y por eso dedica horas a organizar el viaje antes de ir. Primero, busca información online para ver qué tiempo hace en el país en el momento en que quiere ir, y lee información sobre todos los hoteles antes de reservar uno. Además, mira los planos de las ciudades y las páginas de recomendaciones y, después, escribe una lista de todos los sitios que quiere visitar. Y eso no es todo. Cuando vuelve de las vacaciones, crea una presentación con todas sus fotos y comentarios porque le gusta tener un recuerdo de su viaje.

Answer the following questions in **English**.

(a) Why does Sara's mother spend so long on holiday planning?

....

(b) What does she do first?

....

(c) What does she do after looking at maps and recommendations?

....

(d) What does she make when she comes back?

....

(e) Why does she like to do this?

....

(5 marks)

> Skim-reading is a very useful skill. Clues in the questions will give hints to what to look for in the text. For example, in (b), the word 'first' guides you to skim the text until you find the word *primero*. However, once you have found where the answer is likely to be, read the text in detail to make sure you don't miss something.

Had a go ☐ Nearly there ☐ Nailed it! ☐

Media and technology

Computer games

Target grade 1-5

Computer games

1 You are shopping for a videogame with your Spanish friend.

Listen to the recording of the teacher's part. The teacher will play the part of your friend and will speak first.

You should address your friend as *tú*.

When you see this – **?** – you will have to ask a question.

1 Say what you want to buy. (Give **one** detail.)
2 Say who it is for.
3 Say what type of game you want. (Give **one** detail.)
4 Give your opinion of computer games. (Give **one** opinion.)
?5 Ask your friend a question about computer games.

> In order to score full marks, you must include a verb in your response to each task.

> There is often more than one way of saying things, so if you forget one, try to use another. Instead of saying *quiero* for 'I want', two useful alternatives to learn are *me gustaría* and *quisiera*, both of which mean 'I would like'.

(10 marks)

Target grade 7

Computer games

2 You read this article about girls and computer games.

> En el pasado muy pocas chicas jugaban a los videojuegos, pero esto está cambiando rápidamente. Según un informe de la industria, un 46% de los jugadores en el mundo son chicas. Las cifras muestran que las chicas que juegan a juegos sociales en los que cooperan* con amigas tendrán amistades más fuertes después. Es interesante notar que cuando las chicas juegan a un videojuego con mucha violencia sienten más estrés que los chicos. Por eso, aunque muchas chicas eligen jugar a videojuegos de aventura, suelen preferir los que tienen menos violencia.

cooperar – to cooperate

Complete these sentences. Write the letter for the correct option in each box.

(a) The article says that …

A	the gaming industry is targeting girls.
B	more girls play computer games than before.
C	games for girls were poor in the past.

(b) These days …

A	almost half the world's players are female.
B	there are 46% more girl players than ten years ago.
C	more and more games' designers are women.

(c) Girls that play social games …

A	learn to be more competitive.
B	acquire social skills they can use in later life.
C	develop firmer friendships.

(d) Violent games …

A	create more stress in girls than in boys.
B	are just as popular with girls as with boys.
C	can cause violent behaviour in both sexes.

(4 marks)

Media and technology

Had a go ☐ Nearly there ☐ Nailed it! ☐

The good and the bad of technology

Photo card

1 Talk about the content of these photos. You must say at least one thing about each photo.

(5 marks)

After you have spoken about the content of the photos, listen to the recording of further questions on the same topic. Pause the recording for longer if needed to give your answers. There is a sample recording in the Answers section to give you more ideas. **(20 marks)**

> If you are not sure about something in the photo, it's absolutely fine to make a guess. For example, here, the first photo could have been taken in the man's home or in the office. You could start by saying *No estoy seguro/a de dónde está el hombre …* ('I'm not sure where the man is …') and then go on to say that you think he is in his house or in his office.

A technology article

2 You are writing an article about technology.

Write approximately **90** words in **Spanish**.

You must write something about each bullet point.

Mention:
- what you think of technology
- a problem you had with technology last week
- how you will use the internet this weekend.

> Make sure you do not repeat information, as you cannot be credited for it twice. Because you can plan your work in advance, you can think about what information to use for each bullet point ensuring that you don't use the same material twice.

....
....
....
....
....
....
....
....
....
....

(15 marks)

Had a go ☐ **Nearly there** ☐ **Nailed it!** ☐

The environment and where people live

Places in town

Town life

1 You hear this podcast. Iván is talking about where he lives.

   Complete the sentences in **English**.

   Write **one** word in each space.

   (a) Iván lives near the ...., more or less in the .... **(2 marks)**

   (b) He sometimes walks his dog round the .... in the .... **(2 marks)**

   (c) He often goes to the café on the .... to meet his .... **(2 marks)**

Role play

2 You are visiting your Spanish friend and want to go shopping.

   Listen to the recording of the teacher's part. The teacher will play the part of your friend and will speak first.

   You should address your friend as *tú*.

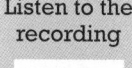

   When you see this – **?** – you will have to ask a question.

   > 1 Say where you want to go and why. (Give **one** place and **one** reason.)
   > 2 Say what you want to buy. (Give **two** details.)
   > 3 Say what else you would like to do in town. (Give **two** details.)
   > 4 Say how you will get there.
   > ?5 Ask your friend a question about eating out.

(10 marks)

> In order to score full marks, you must include a verb in your response to each task.

> If you see a word that you can't remember, or are not sure about, try to think round it so you get a similar message across. For instance, in task 4, we say 'to get there' in English. In Spanish you just need the verb *ir* ('to go'). So you could start by saying *Podemos ir …* ('We can go … ') or *Vamos a ir …* ('Let's go…') and then suggest *a pie* ('on foot') or *en el autobús* ('on the bus').

The environment and where people live

Had a go ☐   Nearly there ☐   Nailed it! ☐

Things to do

Plans for a visit

1. You hear Alejandro telling his cousin, Javier, what they will do when Javier comes to stay. What activity is planned for each day? Where will it take place?

    Write the correct **letter** for the activity. Write the correct **number** for the place.

Listen to the recording

Activity	
A	basketball
B	birthday meal
C	computer games
D	concert
E	film
F	football

Place	
1	a friend's house
2	cinema
3	home
4	park
5	sports centre
6	stadium

                                Activity   Place

(a) Day 1   ☐   ☐   **(2 marks)**

(b) Friday   ☐   ☐   **(2 marks)**

(c) Saturday   ☐   ☐   **(2 marks)**

(d) Sunday   ☐   ☐   **(2 marks)**

> With this type of question, the wording at the start of each sentence gives you a key word to listen out for so that you know that the answer you need is about to be given. Listen out for the word 'first' (*primer / primero*) and the relevant days of the week.

Translation

2. Translate the following sentences into **Spanish**.

    She will go shopping on Tuesday.

> Remember that to say 'on' a day of the week, just use *el* for a singular day and *los* for plural days. 'This' is either *este* (for a masculine singular noun) or *esta* (for a feminine singular noun).

....

He will visit the castle this weekend.

....

I will eat in the café.

....

You will be able to play football on Saturday.

....

I will watch a film in the square.

....

(10 marks)

> The sentences in the exam will mostly be in the present tense, but one will test either the future or the past. Here the sentences are in the future tense to practise the grammar point on page 33 of the Revision Guide.

Had a go ☐   Nearly there ☐   Nailed it! ☐

The environment and where people live

Shopping for clothes

Shopping

1 Read what these people say about shopping. Who says what?

Write **S** for Sara

L for Luisa

J for Javier.

Write the correct letter in each box.

> **Sara:** No entiendo por qué a la gente le gusta ir de compras. El supermercado está bastante lejos de mi casa y siempre está lleno de gente. Por eso nunca voy allí, y hago la compra en la tienda que está al lado de mi casa porque es más práctico.
>
> **Luisa:** Yo no soy aficionada a comprar. Sin embargo, me gusta estar a la moda. Muchos de mis amigos hacen fiestas para vender ropa y maquillaje*, y eso me gusta. ¡Ganan dinero también!
>
> **Javier:** Normalmente compro en las tiendas de uno de los centros comerciales que hay en Burgos. Me encanta la variedad y suelen ser más baratos. ¡Es la mejor manera de comprar! De vez en cuando también compro por Internet.

*maquillaje – make-up

Who …

(a) … likes being in fashion? ☐

(b) … never goes to the supermarket? ☐

(c) … occasionally shops online? ☐

(d) … prefers the local shops? ☐

(e) … enjoys sales parties? ☐

(f) … tends to go to shopping centres? ☐

(6 marks)

Role play

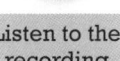

Listen to the recording

2 You are talking to your Mexican friend.

Listen to the recording of the teacher's part. The teacher will play the part of your friend and will speak first.

You should address your friend as *tú*.

When you see this – **?** – you will have to ask a question.

> 1 Say where you go shopping. (Give **one** detail.)
> 2 Say who you prefer to go with. (Give **one** detail.)
> 3 Say what you think of shopping online. (Give **one** opinion.)
> 4 Say what you buy with your money. (Give **one** detail.)
> ?5 Ask your friend a question about shops.

> In order to score full marks, you must include a verb in your response to each task.

(10 marks)

> Some vital verbs that can get you a long way in role plays are these: *quiero* ('I want'), *voy* ('I go / am going'), *me gusta / me gustan* ('I like') and *prefiero* ('I prefer').

The environment and where people live

Had a go ☐ Nearly there ☐ Nailed it! ☐

Transport

Translation

1 Translate these sentences into **English**.

Para ir al instituto antes iba a pie, pero ahora voy en bicicleta.

....

....

Si quiero ir a la ciudad suelo coger el autobús.

....

....

No es tan cómodo como el tren y tarda cuarenta minutos.

....

....

Sin embargo, los billetes son más baratos.

....

....

Se puede tomar un barco para cruzar a la isla.

....

....

(10 marks)

> Remember that *suelo* comes from the verb *soler* and means 'to usually do something'. So if you say *Suelo ir al instituto a pie* you could translate it as 'I usually walk to school.' or 'I usually go to school on foot'.

Photo card

2 Talk about the content of these photos. You must say at least one thing about each photo.

(5 marks)

After you have spoken about the content of the photos, listen to the recording of further questions on the same topic. Pause the recording to give your answers. There is a sample recording in the Answers section to give you more ideas.

(20 marks)

> Don't be afraid to suggest what people might be doing. What are the people doing? Where are they going? Who is the man in the first photo talking to? How do the other people feel about him talking on the phone?

Travelling on public transport

Picture task

1 You decide to send this photo to a friend in Argentina.

> The photo for this task is always in black and white but it's absolutely fine to say what colours you think things are. You can't be wrong!

What is in this photo? Write **five** sentences in **Spanish**.

....
....
....
....
....

(10 marks)

Family trips

2 Listen to this family discussing trips they have made. What opinion does each one express?

Write **P** if the opinion is positive

  N if the opinion is negative

  P+N if the opinion is both positive and negative.

Write the correct letter in each box.

(a) Mother's opinion of the boat trip ☐

(b) Jaime's opinion of the car journey ☐

(c) Olivia's view of train journeys ☐

(d) Father's view of walking ☐

(4 marks)

The environment and where people live

Had a go ☐ Nearly there ☐ Nailed it! ☐

My region – the good and the bad

Dictation

1 You will hear five short sentences. Listen carefully and using your knowledge of Spanish sounds, write down in **Spanish** exactly what you hear for each sentence. You will hear each sentence **three** times: the first time as a full sentence, the second time in short sections and the third time again as a full sentence.

Sentence 1

....

Sentence 2

....

Sentence 3

....

Sentence 4

....

Sentence 5

....

(10 marks)

> In the dictation you have to use your knowledge of the language and the grammar as well as simply recognising individual words. When you hear what sounds like 'athay' you need to remember the letter 'c' sounds like 'th' when it is followed by 'e'. (In fact, the combination of letters 'th' doesn't exist in Spanish!) Then you need to recall the verb *hacer*, with the silent 'h' at the start. Put this knowledge together and you will realise that 'athay' is in fact *hace*.

Where I live

2 You are writing an article about the area where you live.

Write approximately **150** words in **Spanish**.

You must write something about both bullet points.

Mention:

- the pros and cons of the area
- what you did in the area last week.

....

....

> The tasks will make it clear which tenses are required in each bullet point. For example, when it asks you about the pros and cons of the area, you will answer mostly in the present tense. However, you could always show off your knowledge of the future tense in one sentence. Then you will have demonstrated very good language knowledge as you will be using the past tense for the second bullet point.

....

....

....

....

(25 marks)

Continue your answer on your own paper.

Had a go ☐ Nearly there ☐ Nailed it! ☐

The environment and where people live

My region in the past

Reading aloud

1 Read aloud the following text in **Spanish**.

> Mi abuela se acuerda de la ciudad en los años cincuenta.
> Dice que no había mucho tráfico porque casi nadie tenía coche.
> Iban a pie a todas partes.
> La gente trabajaba en la tierra y era bastante pobre.
> El sentido de comunidad era muy fuerte y era una niña feliz.

(5 marks)

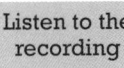

Listen to the recording

Once you have read the text aloud, listen to the **four** recorded questions related to what you have read. Pause the recording after each one to give yourself time to answer.

In order to score the highest marks, you must try to answer all **four** questions as fully as you can.

(10 marks)

> You can check your reading by listening to a recording of the text in the Answers section. You can also hear sample answers to the questions.

> Remember to take care over double vowels. The Spanish combination of '*ie*' is very different to the English. In Spanish you can hear both sounds distinctly: *pie* is pronounced 'pee – eh'. In English 'ie' in 'pie' just sounds like 'eye'.

Translation

2 Translate the following sentences into **Spanish**.

There are lots of fields in my region.

....

We do not have green spaces in the city.

....

The neighbours in my street are very friendly.

....

I like the park next to the river.

....

I used to live in a small village.

....

(10 marks)

> If a verb in the past is one word, you are likely to need the preterite tense ('we went, I saw, they found'). If it says 'used to' (as in question (e)) or 'was / were …ing' you will need the imperfect.

The environment and where people live

Had a go ☐ Nearly there ☐ Nailed it! ☐

Town or country?

Where we live

1 Héctor and Laura are talking about where they live. What do they say?

Write **A** if only statement A is correct

B if only statement B is correct

A+B if both statements A and B are correct.

(a) Héctor says that Gandía …

A	is in the southeast of Spain.
B	has sixty thousand inhabitants.

(b) Gandía …

A	was a lot greener in the past.
B	gets a lot of tourists.

(c) Héctor thinks …

A	they need more hotels.
B	they need more green spaces.

(d) Laura says that the island where she lives …

A	is very popular with visitors.
B	has forty thousand inhabitants.

(e) The island has …

A	a network of buses.
B	plenty of transport for all.

(f) Laura thinks …

A	transport is not a priority.
B	the environment is more important.

(6 marks)

> Be careful with numbers. It is easy to confuse *seis* ('six') and *siete* ('seven'), and *sesenta* ('sixty') with *setenta* ('seventy'). Also, make sure that you have heard the **whole** number. Laura says that there are **ciento** *cuarenta mil* inhabitants not just *cuarenta mil*.

The north coast of Spain

2 Read this extract from a tourist brochure.

> La costa del norte parece ser un secreto bien guardado porque es preciosa, pero es una zona poco visitada por los turistas extranjeros. Sin embargo, muchos españoles han descubierto sus ventajas y vienen a la región para buscar la paz del campo y estar en contacto con la naturaleza. Aquí hay de todo, desde maravillosas playas de arena hasta montañas muy altas. No muy lejos de la costa encontrarás numerosas ciudades históricas que vale la pena visitar.

Complete these sentences. Write the letter for the correct option in each box.

(a) The north coast is described as …

A	touristy.
B	beautiful.
C	rainy.

(b) The area …

A	is popular with foreign tourists.
B	gets few visitors.
C	is appreciated by Spanish visitors.

(c) People go there to …

A	go camping.
B	get in touch with nature.
C	escape the heat.

(d) The article mentions …

A	small villages.
B	sandy beaches.
C	green fields.

(e) The cities are …

A	not far from the coast.
B	there on the coast.
C	a long way inland.

(5 marks)

Had a go ☐ **Nearly there** ☐ **Nailed it!** ☐

The environment and where people live

The environment and me

Helping the environment

1. You are writing to your friend about helping the environment.

   Write approximately **90** words in **Spanish**.

   You must write something about each bullet point. Mention:
   - your opinion of public transport in your area
   - what you did to help the environment last week
   - what you are going to do in the future to save energy.

   > In the Writing paper, the aim is to show off your Spanish so don't worry if you have to bend the truth a little in order to complete the task. Use the vocabulary you know and adapt it to the task as required.

   ....
   ....
   ....
   ....
   ....
   ....
   ....
   ....
   ....

   (15 marks)

Translation

2. Translate the following sentences into **Spanish**.

   It is very important to protect the planet.

   ....
   ....

   We must do what we can to care for the environment.

   ....
   ....

   In our house, we usually recycle paper, bottles and plastic.

   ....
   ....

   When I went out last week, I used public transport.

   ....
   ....

   My sister is going to take her clothes to a second-hand shop.

   ....
   ....

   (10 marks)

   > When 'what?' is a question use *¿qué?*
   >
   > When 'what' is not a question (as in the second sentence) use *lo que*.
   >
   > To translate *second-hand shop,* be careful of the word order. It will be 'shop of second hand', and remember that *mano* is feminine.

81

 **The environment and where people live**

Had a go ☐ Nearly there ☐ Nailed it! ☐

Local environmental issues

 Target grade 4-9

Picture task

1 Talk about the content of these photos. You must say at least one thing about each photo.

(5 marks)

After you have spoken about the content of the photos, listen to the recording of further questions on the same topic. Pause the recording to give your answers. There is a sample recording in the Answers section to give you more ideas.

(20 marks)

> In these pictures, you can talk about the teams or groups of young people who are working to help or care for the environment. You could talk about the T-shirts they wear and the actions of picking up rubbish and planting trees. You can describe where you think they are – perhaps parks in the city. Don't forget the weather and even your opinion of what they are doing.

 Target grade 1-5

Translation

2 Translate the following sentences into **Spanish**.

There is a lot of pollution in the sea.

....

I like the green spaces in the city.

....

We are going to walk to town.

....

My mother hated the noise from the road.

....

The air is cleaner in the countryside.

....

(10 marks)

> To create the comparative adjective 'cleaner than' you need to say 'more clean than'.
>
> 'Clean' still agrees with its noun ('air') and the verb to use with 'clean' is *estar*. To say 'than', you need *que*.

Had a go ☐   Nearly there ☐   Nailed it! ☐

The environment and where people live

Global environmental issues

A disaster in the south

1 Julia and Miguel are talking about an environmental issue.
   What do they say? Write the correct letter in each box.

(a) Miguel asks if Julia has heard about the …

A	fires.
B	floods.
C	accident.

(b) Julia says that many people …

A	are without power.
B	are stranded.
C	are homeless.

(c) Miguel says that …

A	no one was killed.
B	many are injured.
C	people are missing.

Remember that you will hear the listening recordings twice, with built-in pauses. Try to just listen the first time through. You can make notes in the gaps or immediately afterwards but concentrating on listening intently will ensure you grasp the gist of the recording and alert you to the important bits of the conversation.

(3 marks)

Dictation

2 You will now hear five short sentences. Listen carefully and using your knowledge of Spanish sounds, write down in **Spanish** exactly what you hear for each sentence. You will hear each sentence **three** times: the first time as a full sentence, the second time in short sections and the third time again as a full sentence.

Sentence 1

....

Sentence 2

....

Sentence 3

....

Sentence 4

....

Sentence 5

....

(10 marks)

Remember that the sound 'kwa' is always spelt *cua* in Spanish (as in *cuatro*) and never 'qua' as we do in English. Also, if you hear what sounds like 'tha' (with a soft 'th' like in Na**th**an) it will be *za* in Spanish. The combination of letters 't + h' does not exist in Spanish.

83

The environment and where people live

Had a go ☐   Nearly there ☐   Nailed it! ☐

Caring for the planet

An environmental forum

1 You read these comments on an internet forum about the environment.

> Mañana voy a estar con un grupo de ciudadanos que están enojados. Participamos en una manifestación contra la falta de acción del gobierno en el tema de la contaminación del aire de la ciudad.
> *Andrés*
>
> Me preocupa mucho que los jefes de gobierno mundiales no hagan bastante para resolver el problema del cambio climático. Si las temperaturas siguen subiendo, vamos a tener condiciones que amenazan la vida de la gente.
> *Bea*
>
> Quiero dar las gracias al grupo de jóvenes que se ofrecieron a limpiar el río. Ahora las aguas están puras y sanas y he visto la vuelta de pájaros a la zona.
> *Carlos*

Who says what?

Write **A** for Andrés
       B for Bea
       C for Carlos.

Write the correct letter in each box.

> When you answer question (b), you may notice that both Andrés and Bea complain about the authorities not taking enough action. However, only one of them is talking about world leaders; the other is talking about local government.

Who …

(a) … is grateful to a band of volunteers? ☐

(b) … feels that world leaders are not doing enough? ☐

(c) … is taking part in a protest march? ☐

(d) … has seen nature return to a once-polluted area? ☐

(e) … is concerned about breathing contaminated air? ☐

(f) … believes the changing climate is a threat to life? ☐

(6 marks)

Reading aloud

2 Amaya, your Chilean friend, writes about the environment where she lives.

Read aloud the text below.

> La zona donde vivo no sufre problemas de contaminación.
> Aquí en las montañas el aire es muy puro.
> Tenemos una gran cantidad de especies de animales y pájaros.
> Pero abajo en algunas partes han cortado muchos árboles.
> En la ciudad se nota el humo y el ruido de la industria.

> Remember that the letter 'h' is not pronounced at all. You should not hear the slightest breath at the beginning of words like *han* and *humo*. Pretend that the 'h' is not even there.

(5 marks)

Listen to the recording

Once you have read the text aloud, listen to the **four** recorded questions related to what you have read. Pause the recording after each one to give yourself time to answer.

In order to score the highest marks, you must try to answer all **four** questions as fully as you can.

(10 marks)

Had a go ☐   Nearly there ☐   Nailed it! ☐   **The environment and where people live**

A greener future

Photo card

1 Talk about the content of these photos. You must say at least **one** thing about each photo.

Photo 1

Photo 2

(5 marks)

After you have spoken about the content of the photos, listen to the recording of further questions on the same topic. Pause the recording to give your answers. There is a sample recording in the Answers section to give you more ideas.

(20 marks)

> These children could be in a park (*un parque*) or in the countryside (*el campo*). In photo 1, they could be studying nature (*la naturaleza*) or learning about trees and flowers (*árboles y flores*). In photo 2, they are learning how to look after trees (*están aprendiendo a cuidar los árboles*).

Translation

2 Translate the following sentences into **Spanish**.

The sun, the wind and the sea create a lot of energy.

....

....

It is clean energy that causes less pollution.

....

....

I read this information online yesterday.

....

....

I believe that the government need to spend more on developing these resources.

....

....

It will be much better for the future of the planet.

....

....

(10 marks)

> 'We will be able' is the future tense of the verb *poder*. Remember that it has an irregular stem in the future, it loses an 'e'. Normally, the future endings are added to the infinitive, but some verbs lose the 'e' of the infinitive ending like *poder* (**podr**...), *saber* (**sabr**...) and *querer* (**querr**...)

About the exams

Had a go ☐ Nearly there ☐ Nailed it! ☐

Practice for Paper 1: Listening

Practise for the Listening tasks with this selection of exam-style questions.

Target grade 2

Track 95

Eating out

1. Amira is talking about a meal she had in a restaurant.

   What does she say?

   Write the correct letter in the box.

   (a) Amira thought the vegetarian food ...

A	had too much salt.
B	was very tasty.
C	was a bit boring.

   (b) Amira did not like ...

A	the bread.
B	the fish.
C	the meat.

   (2 marks)

Target grade 3

Track 96

TV programmes

2. David is talking about what he watches on TV.

   Which **three** type of programmes does David mention?

   Write the correct letters in the boxes.

A	music
B	sport
C	history
D	films
E	cooking
F	travel

   > You can use the space to the right of the grid to tick any words that you hear while you are listening. A quick tick will not stop you listening to the recording.

   (3 marks)

Target grade 5

Track 97

A festival

3. Listen to Natalia talking in a podcast.

   Where are these events happening?

A	bullring
B	high street
C	park
D	port
E	square
F	stadium

   > Listen to all the recording. Don't jump to conclusions on the basis of one word.

   Write the correct letter in each box.

   (a) Most events are in the ...

   (b) Children's games are in the ...

   (c) The market is in the ...

   (3 marks)

Had a go ☐ Nearly there ☐ Nailed it! ☐   **About the exams**

Practice for Paper 1: Listening

Practise for the Listening tasks with this selection of exam-style questions.

Studying

1 Sofía and Carlos are talking about their studies. Complete the sentences in **English**. Write **one** word in each space.

Example: Sofía likes <u>group</u> activities because she <u>learns</u> more this way.

(a) Sofía hates .... because she finds the
    exercises ....   **(2 marks)**

(b) Carlos likes .... at 2:30, but believes
    the .... is very expensive.   **(2 marks)**

Dictation

2 You will now hear five short sentences.

Listen carefully and using your knowledge of Spanish sounds, write down in **Spanish** exactly what you hear for each sentence.

You will hear each sentence **three** times: the first time as a full sentence, the second time in short sections and the third time again as a full sentence.

Sentence 1

....

....

Sentence 2

....

....

Sentence 3

....

....

Sentence 4

....

....

Sentence 5

....

....   **(10 marks)**

Use your knowledge of Spanish sounds and grammar to make sure that what you have written makes sense. Remember to check carefully that your spelling is accurate.

About the exams

Had a go ☐ Nearly there ☐ Nailed it! ☐

Practice for Paper 2: Speaking

Practise for the Speaking tasks with this selection of exam-style questions.

Reading aloud

1 Read aloud the following text in **Spanish**.

> En mi ciudad el aire no está muy limpio porque hay mucha contaminación de los coches.
>
> También se puede ver basura en las calles.
>
> El medio ambiente es mejor en otoño después de las lluvias.

Track 100

Now play the recording to listen to and answer four questions in Spanish that relate to the topic of **The environment and where people live**. In order to score the highest marks, you must try to **answer all four questions as fully as you can**.

You can hear a sample recording of the text, questions and answers in the Answers section.

> When you get 'a' and 'i' together, as in *aire*, they do not sound like the English word 'air'. They sound like a combination of 'a' and 'i' and make a sound like 'eye'.

Reading aloud

2 Read aloud the following text in **Spanish**.

> Soy hijo único y vivo en una ciudad en el oeste de España.
>
> Mi padre es policía y mi madre es jefa de ventas en una compañía de seguridad.
>
> Los dos tienen cuarenta y cinco años.
>
> Normalmente, me llevo muy bien con ellos porque tenemos el mismo sentido del humor.

Track 101

Now play the recording to listen to and answer four questions in Spanish that relate to the topic of **Identity and relationships with others**. In order to score the highest marks, you must try to **answer all four questions as fully as you can**.

You can hear a sample recording of the text, questions and answers in the Answers section.

> Remember that if a word has an accent, that is where the word should be stressed: *único / policía / compañía*.

Had a go ☐ Nearly there ☐ Nailed it! ☐   **About the exams**

Practice for Paper 2: Speaking

Practise for the Speaking tasks with this selection of exam-style questions.

Target grade 4-9

Role play

Track 102

1 You are talking to your Spanish friend.

Listen to the recording of the teacher's part. The teacher will play the part of your friend and will speak first.

You should address your friend as *tú*.

When you see this – ? – you will have to ask a question.

> 1 Say what exercise you do. (Give **two** details.)
> 2 Say what healthy food you eat. (Give **one** detail.)
> 3 Say what you avoid eating. (Give **two** details.)
> ?4 Ask your friend a question about vegetarian food.
> 5 Say what you will do to relax at the weekend. (Give **two** details.)

> If you cannot remember 'vegetarian' you could ask if they eat vegetables, or fruit, or rice, or meals without meat, etc.

(10 marks)

> In order to score full marks, you must include at least one verb in your response to each task.

Target grade 4-9

Photo card

2 Look at the two photos as part of your preparation. Make as many notes as you want on an Additional Answer Sheet for use during the test.

Talk about the content of the photos. The recommended time is approximately one and half minutes at Higher tier. You must say at least one thing about each photo.

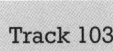
Track 103

After you have spoken about the content of the photos, play the recording to hear and respond to questions related to any of the topics within the theme of **Communication and the world around us**.

(25 marks)

> For the first photo, you could mention clean sand, hot weather, blue sky and buildings in the distance. For photo two, you could mention that it is a different type of holiday, a cultural visit to historic places.

Practice for Paper 3: Reading

Practise for the Reading tasks with this selection of exam-style questions.

Food and drink

1 Read these online restaurant reviews.

> **Carla:** Fuimos al restaurante para celebrar el cumpleaños de mi madre. Nos gustó mucho toda la comida y pasamos una tarde muy buena.
> **Daniel:** Había una oferta especial cuando fuimos y la comida fue bastante barata. Sin embargo, sirvieron café frío al final de la cena.
> **Mónica:** Tienen una lista de platos principales muy ricos. Por otra parte, los postres no son muy interesantes, una naranja, una manzana, **flan** y poco más.

Who says what? Write the correct letter in each box.

Write   **C** for Carla
        D for Daniel
        M for Mónica.

Who …

(a) thought the list of main dishes was great? ☐ (1 mark)

(b) was there for a family event? ☐ (1 mark)

(c) found the desserts disappointing? ☐ (1 mark)

(d) thought the price was reasonable? ☐ (1 mark)

(e) Read the last sentence again. What is *flan*?

| A | A type of salad | B | A type of dessert | C | A type of main dish |

☐ (1 mark)

Places in town

2 You read Manuel's email.

> ✉
> Recuerda que mañana es un día de fiesta y el supermercado estará cerrado. Si necesitas ir de compras, debes ir hoy. El sábado recomiendo una exposición de arte en el pueblo. Si te interesa ir, podemos verla juntos e ir de tapas después. ¿Qué te parece?

Complete these sentences. Write the letter for the correct option in each box.

(a) You should go shopping …

A	today.
B	tomorrow.
C	on Saturday.

☐

(b) He recommends going to …

A	a parade in town.
B	a celebrity football match.
C	an art exhibition.

☐

(c) Afterwards, he suggests …

A	seeing a film.
B	eating out.
C	going for a drink.

☐

(3 marks)

Had a go ☐   Nearly there ☐   Nailed it! ☐   **About the exams**

Practice for Paper 3: Reading

Practise for the Reading tasks with this selection of exam-style questions.

Future opportunities

1 Read this extract from a webpage about voluntary work on a farm in South America.

Trabajo A	**Trabajar con animales** – aprenderás a cuidar de los caballos. Por las tardes, podrás ayudar en las clases cuando los niños vienen a aprender a montar a caballo.
Trabajo B	**Trabajar en una granja*** – ayudarás en los campos a recoger las *piñas* cuando están listas. Los viernes, estarás en la tienda vendiendo todas las frutas que tenemos.
Trabajo C	**Trabajar con turistas** – por la mañana estarás con la gente que visita la granja explicando el trabajo que hacemos. Por la tarde los acompañarás en una excursión y explicarás la historia de la región.

*granja – farm

Answer the following questions in **English**.

Job A

(a) What will you learn to do? .... **(1 mark)**

(b) What will your afternoon task be? .... **(1 mark)**

Job B

(c) What will your Friday job be? .... **(1 mark)**

Job C

(d) What will your morning job be? .... **(1 mark)**

(e) What will your role be during the trip? .... **(1 mark)**

(f) Read Job **B** again. What are *piñas*?

| A | fruit | B | vegetables | C | flowers |

(1 mark)

Translation

2 Translate these sentences into **English**.

Reciclamos el vidrio y el papel cada semana.

....

El vuelo sale a las once y media de la mañana el jueves.

....

Estoy muy feliz porque aprobé el examen de informática.

....

El número de accidentes aumentará si no resolvemos el problema.

....

El alumno fue castigado por romper las reglas varias veces.

....

(10 marks)

91

About the exams

Had a go ☐ Nearly there ☐ Nailed it! ☐

Practice for Paper 4: Writing

Practise for the Reading tasks with this selection of exam-style questions.

Picture task

1 You send this photo to a friend in Argentina.

What is in this photo? Write five sentences in **Spanish**.

....
....
....
....
....

(10 marks)

Writing an email

2 Write an email to your Chilean friend about shopping.

Write approximately **50** words in **Spanish**. You must write something about each bullet point.

Mention:

- when you go
- where you go
- who you go with
- opinion of the shops
- what you buy.

> Opinions can use phrases like *Me gusta …, Me encanta …, Odio …* or adjectives like *bonito, excelente, interesante, terrible, genial.*

(10 marks)

....
....
....
....
....

Grammar task

3 Using your knowledge of grammar, complete the following sentences in **Spanish**. Choose the correct Spanish word from the three options in the grid. Write the correct word in the space.

(a) Vamos a visitar a .... abuela esta tarde.

nuestro	nuestros	nuestra

(b) Me gusta .... al cine con mis amigos.

salgo	salir	saliendo

(c) Normalmente yo .... los deberes a las seis.

hago	hacer	haces

(d) Mi casa .... cerca del centro de la ciudad.

es	están	está

(e) La primera clase .... día empieza a las nueve.

de	del	al

(5 marks)

Had a go ☐   Nearly there ☐   Nailed it! ☐   **About the exams**

Practice for Paper 4: Writing

Practise for the Writing tasks with this selection of exam-style questions.

Translation

1 Translate the following sentences into **Spanish**.

To have a healthy lifestyle, it is important to do exercise.

....

....

I am going to get up early tomorrow.

....

....

When I was on holiday, I watched a film in the open air.

....

....

The computer is broken and I cannot do my homework.

....

....

A Spanish singer won the European competition last year.

....

.... **(10 marks)**

> The first sentence starts with 'To have' which is another way of saying 'In order to have'. When the phrase 'in order to' is implied, you will need the word *para* in Spanish. In the third sentence, you will need the imperfect tense for 'I was'.

Writing an email

2 You are writing an email to your friend about education and work.

Write approximately **90** words in **Spanish**. You must write something about each bullet point. Mention:

- your opinion of studying languages
- what you did to prepare for your last exams
- the type of job that you want to do in the future.

....

....

....

....

....

....

.... **(15 marks)**

Grammar

Had a go ☐ Nearly there ☐ Nailed it! ☐

Nouns and articles

> Remember not all words ending in *a* are feminine or ending in *o* are masculine! There are exceptions.

1. Write the correct definite article *el, la, los, las*.

   Example: la gente

   (a) .... mesa
   (b) .... fútbol
   (c) .... patatas fritas
   (d) .... dientes
   (e) .... mano
   (f) .... piso
   (g) .... ciencias
   (h) .... restaurantes
   (i) .... problema
   (j) .... foto

2. Complete the sentences with either the definite article *el, la, los, las* or the indefinite article *un, una*.
   Remember to think about gender and whether it is singular or plural.

   Example: En casa tengo un perro que es negro y blanco.

   (a) En mi opinión, las verduras son más ricas que .... frutas.
   (b) En mi casa hay .... cuarto de baño y tres dormitorios.
   (c) No me gusta nada .... francés porque es complicado.
   (d) Todos .... martes tengo club de baile.
   (e) En la mesa hay .... regla y tres bolígrafos.
   (f) Mi instituto es grande y hay .... campo de deportes.
   (g) Me he roto .... pie y me duele mucho.
   (h) .... domingo fuimos a una piscina al aire libre cerca de mi casa.

> We sometimes use articles in English when they are not needed in Spanish, for example:
> 1 when talking about jobs
> 2 after *sin* and *con*.
>
> We sometimes use articles in Spanish when they are not needed in English, for example:
> 1 talking generally (with a noun at the start of a sentence)
> 2 to express opinions
> 3 before days of the week (*el lunes voy a ...*).

3. Read the sentences and cross out any articles that have been used where they are not needed.

   Example: No tengo ~~un~~ coche porque prefiero viajar en metro.

   (a) Vivo en un piso cómodo en las afueras.
   (b) Mi padre es un policía y mi madre es una médica.
   (c) Hay muy pocos estudiantes en el instituto sin un móvil.
   (d) Escribo con un bolígrafo en mi clase de matemáticas.
   (e) En el futuro me gustaría ser una actriz.
   (f) El deporte es muy importante para llevar una vida sana.
   (g) Odio las clases de música porque no puedo cantar bien.
   (h) Se puede reservar dos habitaciones con una ducha.

Had a go ☐ **Nearly there** ☐ **Nailed it!** ☐ **Grammar**

Adjectives

> Most adjectives agree as follows:
> end in **–o**: al**to** / al**ta** / al**tos** / al**tas**
> end in **–e**: add **–s** in the plural
> end in **consonant***: add **–es** in the plural
> *Nationalities also have a separate feminine singular form: *español**a***

1 Find the correct adjective from the list. Remember that the adjective must agree with the noun.

   Example: una mujer seria

   (a) una cama ....
   (b) dos gatos ....
   (c) un vestido ....
   (d) las películas son ....
   (e) el profesor es ....
   (f) las actrices son ....
   (g) la playa es ....
   (h) nuestros coches son ....

   | cómoda |
   | baratos |
   | español |
   | interesantes |
   | bonita |
   | rojo |
   | ~~seria~~ |
   | simpáticas |
   | contentos |

2 Choose the correct adjective.

   Example: Vivo en un piso muy *pequeña* / (*pequeño*) / *pequeños*.

   (a) Me quedé en un hotel *moderno* / *moderna* / *modernos* de cuatro estrellas.
   (b) Me gusta llevar pantalones *cómodas* / *cómodos* / *cómodo*.
   (c) Creo que mi instituto es bastante *bueno* / *buen* / *buena*.
   (d) La información era *emocionantes* / *emocionante* / *emocionan*.
   (e) La estación de tren está siempre *limpia* / *limpio* / *limpias*.
   (f) Me encantan las ciencias porque son muy *útiles* / *útil* / *utilizas*.

> Some adjectives have shortened forms which are positioned before the noun:
> *un coche bueno* → *un buen coche*

3 Write out these sentences with the correct adjective in the correct place.

   Example: Suelo comer fruta porque es sana y muy rica. (mucho / mucha)
   Suelo comer mucha fruta porque es sana y muy rica.

   (a) En Inglaterra hay gente que habla muy bien alemán. (poco / poca)

   ....

   (b) Lo mejor es que tiene un jardín. (bonito / bonita)

   ....

   (c) Estamos porque hace buen tiempo. (contento / contentas)

   ....

   (d) En el futuro habrá una estación en las afueras de la ciudad. (gran / grandes)

   ....

   (e) Mi abuela vive en el piso. (primera / primer)

   ....

Grammar

Had a go ☐ Nearly there ☐ Nailed it! ☐

Possessives and pronouns

1 Complete the table with the missing possessive adjectives.

English	Spanish singular	Spanish plural
my	mi	
your		tus
his / her / its		
our		nuestros / nuestras
your		
their	su	

2 Complete each sentence with the correct possessive adjective.

(a) My house is big. .... casa es grande.

(b) His brother is the oldest. .... hermano es el mayor.

(c) Their sons play basketball. .... hijos juegan al baloncesto.

(d) My favourite films are science fiction. .... películas preferidas son las de ciencia ficción.

(e) Its food is healthy. .... comida es sana.

> Possessive pronouns are like possessive adjectives but replace the noun they describe. They must agree with the noun they replace!
>
> In Spanish they are always accompanied by the definite article:
>
> | el mío / la mía / los míos / las mías = mine | el tuyo / la tuya = yours |
> |---|---|
> | el suyo / la suya = his / hers | el nuestro / la nuestra = ours |

3 Complete these comparisons with the correct possessive pronoun.

Example: Nuestras fotos no son tan buenas como las tuyas. (yours)
(Our photos are not as good as yours.)

(a) Tu perro es más listo que .... (mine)

(b) Mis gafas son menos grandes que .... (his)

(c) Tu profesor de historia es más estricto que .... (ours)

(d) Su uniforme es más cómodo que .... (yours)

4 Rewrite the phrases to create one sentence using the relative pronoun *que*.

Example: Tengo un hermano. Se llama Diego ⟶ Tengo un hermano que se llama Diego.

(a) María tiene un gato. Es negro y pequeño.

....

(b) Vivimos en un pueblo. Está en el norte del país.

....

(c) En la clase de inglés tengo que leer un libro. Es muy aburrido.

....

Had a go ☐ Nearly there ☐ Nailed it! ☐   **Grammar**

Comparisons

> To form the comparative: **más** + adjective + **que** = more ... than
> **menos** + adjective + **que** = less ... than
> **tan** + adjective + **como** = as ... as

1 Read the English and then complete each Spanish sentence with the correct comparative adjective.

Example: My sister is taller than my brother.
Mi hermana es más alta que mi hermano.

(a) My mother is taller than my father.
Mi madre es .... mi padre.

(b) Marta is less serious than Francisco.
Marta es .... Francisco.

(c) This bus is slower than the train.
Este autobús es .... el tren.

(d) Fruit is as healthy as vegetables.
La fruta es .... las verduras.

(e) This shirt is as expensive as that dress.
Esta camisa es .... aquel vestido.

> Remember!
> el / la mejor, los / las mejores = the best
> el / la peor, los / las peores = the worst

2 Write out the correct superlative sentence.

Example: Esta falda es la menos cara. (the least expensive)

(a) Mi profesor de inglés es .... (the best)

(b) Mis deberes de religión son .... (the worst)

(c) Mi mejor amiga es .... de la clase. (the smallest)

(d) Estas novelas son .... (the most difficult)

(e) Las películas de acción son .... (the least boring)

3 Translate these sentences into **Spanish**.

> To translate words like 'incredibly' or 'extremely' don't forget to use the ending -ísimo/a.

Example: My car is the cheapest. Mi coche es el más barato.

(a) My cousin is stronger than your uncle. ....

(b) Her mobile phone is incredibly small. ....

(c) The Spanish exam is extremely easy. ....

(d) Adventure films are as exciting as action films. ....

(e) My school is the oldest! ....

(f) Science is less boring than geography. ....

(g) My friend Martín is our best player. ....

Grammar

Had a go ☐   Nearly there ☐   Nailed it! ☐

Other adjectives

> Demonstrative adjectives are used to indicate which thing / person you are referring to ('this', 'those' etc). There are three in Spanish: one for 'this / these' and one for 'that / those'. Another version, meaning 'that / those further away' is needed at Higher level only. All forms agree with their noun in number and gender.

1 Complete the table with the correct demonstrative adjective.

English	Masculine singular	Feminine singular	Masculine plural	Feminine plural
this / these	este			
that / those		esa		
that (over there) / those (over there)			aquellos	

2 Translate into **Spanish**. (o/t = 'over there')

(a) these t-shirts ....
(b) this t-shirt ....
(c) that girl (o/t) .... [H only]
(d) those eggs ....
(e) that mobile phone ....
(f) those magazines (o/t) .... [H only]
(g) this book ....
(h) that film ....
(i) that train (o/t) .... [H only]
(j) these plates ....
(k) those oranges ....
(l) those boys (o/t) .... [H only]

3 Complete the sentences with the correct indefinite adjectives from the box below.

> cada   todo / toda   algún / alguna   otro / otra
> mismo / misma   todos / todas   algunos / algunas
> otros / otras   mismos / mismas

(a) Juega al baloncesto .... (every) día.
(b) Siempre da la .... (same) opinión.
(c) Conozco a .... (some) chicos que trabajan de peluqueros.
(d) Ayer, ... (all) los alumnos hicieron sus exámenes.
(e) Voy a hablar con Pablo porque él tiene .... (another) mochila.

4 Fill in the gaps in the text using both demonstrative and indefinite adjectives. The text is translated for you below.

> El año pasado fui de vacaciones con mi familia. (a) .... los años vamos al sur de Inglaterra, pero este año fuimos a España. (b) .... de mis amigos han ido a España, pero esta fue mi primera vez. ¡Me gustó mucho! (c) .... los españoles que conocimos eran muy simpáticos y (d) .... hablaban muy bien inglés. En España, a los jóvenes les gusta la (e) .... ropa que a los jóvenes ingleses y nos divierten las (f) .... actividades. ¡Fue muy interesante!

> Last year I went on holiday with my family. Every year we go to the South of England but this year we went to Spain. Some of my friends have been to Spain but this was my first time. I liked it a lot! All the Spanish people we met were really nice and some spoke very good English. In Spain, the young people love the same clothes as English young people and we like the same activities. It was really interesting!

Had a go ☐ Nearly there ☐ Nailed it! ☐

Pronouns

1 Complete the table with the correct subject pronouns in **English** or **Spanish**.

yo	
	you singular
	he
ella	

	we (masc.)
nosotras	
vosotros	
	you plural (fem.)
ellos	
	they (fem.)

> A pronoun replaces a noun. An object pronoun has the action (shown by the verb) done to it. It can be direct or indirect.
>
> She sent it to me. – **it** = direct object; **me** = indirect object
>
> Direct object pronouns: *me*, *te*, *lo / la*, *nos*, *os*, *los / las*
>
> Position of the object pronouns:
> - Before a conjugated verb: *lo compro* (I buy it), *lo he comprado* (I have bought it)
> - After a negative: *no lo compro* (I don't buy it)
> - At the end of an infinitive or gerund (or before the verb): *voy a comprarlo / lo voy a comprar* (I am going to buy it), *estoy comprándolo / lo estoy comprando* (I am buying it)

2 Replace the noun with the correct object pronoun.

Example: Miguel ha perdido la maleta. → Miguel la ha perdido.

(a) Hemos perdido las mochilas. ....

(b) Han perdido la foto. ....

(c) Teresa come el bocadillo. ....

(d) Compro el vestido. ....

(e) No bebo leche. ....

(f) No lavo la ropa. ....

(g) Quiero escribir un correo electrónico. ....

(h) No quiero leer esa novela. ....

> Indirect object pronouns: *me*, *te*, *le*, *nos*, *os*, *les*

3 Translate these sentences, which use direct and indirect object pronouns, into **English** or **Spanish**.

Example: Le di mi libro de matemáticas. → I gave him my Maths book.

(a) Le voy a escribir esta tarde. ....

(b) Los visité ayer. ....

(c) Lo haré si tengo tiempo. ....

(d) Le di un regalo para su cumpleaños. ....

(e) ¿Las has visto? ....

(f) She came to visit me at home. ....

(g) They sent me the information. ....

(h) I am going to buy them (masc.) online. ....

Grammar — Had a go ☐ Nearly there ☐ Nailed it! ☐

The present tense

> To form the present tense, replace the infinitive ending with:
>
> *–ar* verbs: **o**, **as**, **a**, **amos**, **áis**, **an**
>
> *–er* verbs: **o**, **es**, **e**, **emos**, **éis**, **en**
>
> *–ir* verbs: **o**, **es**, **e**, **imos**, **ís**, **en**
>
> *Tú* is used for people you know and in the present tense the verb will always end in *s*.
>
> *Usted* is the formal word for 'you' and the verb takes the same ending as *él* or *ella*, and therefore has no *s* at the end.

1. Write the verb in the correct person.

   Example: escuchar (tú) → *escuchas*

   (a) vivir (nosotros) → ....
   (b) bailar (ellas) → ....
   (c) vender (yo) → ....
   (d) llevar (vosotros) → ....
   (e) odiar (tú) → ....
   (f) comer (él) → ....
   (g) salir (nosotros) → ....
   (h) escuchar (usted) → ....

2. Choose the correct verb for each sentence.

   Example: En mi tiempo libre (*practico*) / *practican* deportes.

   (a) Mis padres *comemos* / *comen* mucha carne.
   (b) Mi hermana y yo *vive* / *vivimos* en un barrio bonito.
   (c) ¿A qué hora *tienes* / *tienen* tu clase de baile?
   (d) Solo *habla* / *hablan* en francés cuando están solos.
   (e) Usted *debes* / *debe* escribir aquí.
   (f) Nuestro profesor es simpático y nunca *grita* / *gritáis*.
   (g) Normalmente *hablas* / *hablo* con mis amigos por Internet.
   (h) A veces su profesor *lee* / *leen* en clase.
   (i) ¿Usted qué *piensa* / *pensáis* del precio de la ropa?
   (j) *Puedes* / *Podéis* comprar vuestros billetes aquí.

3. Write the correct part of the verb in each sentence. Watch out for radical-changing verbs!

   Example: Mis amigos *estudian* inglés, francés y español. (estudiar)

   (a) Nos gusta la comida española y esta noche .... tapas. (cenar)
   (b) Los artistas a veces .... al aire libre. (trabajar)
   (c) Me levanto temprano y .... el desayuno a las ocho y media. (tomar)
   (d) Limpia su dormitorio y luego .... la mesa. (poner)
   (e) Nunca comemos caramelos, pero .... patatas fritas a menudo. (comprar)
   (f) ¿Cuánto .... las verduras? (costar)
   (g) .... un teléfono móvil, pero no tengo dinero. (querer)
   (h) Los niños .... mucho hoy en día. (pedir)

Had a go ☐ Nearly there ☐ Nailed it! ☐   **Grammar**

Reflexive verbs

1 Write the correct reflexive pronouns next to each part of the verb *levantarse* and *sentirse*.

	levanto
te	levantas
	levanta
	levantamos
	levantáis
se	levantan

	siento
	sientes
	siente
	sentimos
	sentís
	sienten

2 Complete the sentences with the correct reflexive pronoun.

Example: A veces mis amigos no *se* visten bien.

(a) Normalmente, los sábados .... levanta a las nueve y media.

(b) Mis hermanos no .... llevan bien, pero yo me llevo bien con ellos.

(c) ¿............ sientes bien ahora?

(d) Los niños .... parecen mucho a su padre.

(e) Mis primos .... llaman John y Emma.

(f) .... levantamos temprano para ir de vacaciones.

(g) ¿Qué día .... casáis?

(h) .... lavas y te vistes antes de ir al colegio.

3 Rewrite the story for Olivia. Change all the verbs in the 'I' form to the 'she' form. Don't forget to change the non-reflexive verbs too!

> Todos los días me levanto temprano para ir a trabajar. Trabajo en una tienda de ropa famosa. Primero me lavo y me visto. Bajo la escalera y tomo el desayuno. Siempre me siento en la cocina para comer. Después, me lavo la cara en el cuarto de baño que está abajo, al lado de la cocina. Me pongo los zapatos y salgo a las ocho y media porque el autobús llega a las nueve menos cuarto. Vuelvo a casa a las siete de la tarde.

Todos los días Olivia se levanta

....

....

....

....

....

....

....

....

> Remember! Some verbs are regular but have an irregular ending in the first person singular. *Poner* is one of those verbs: *pongo, pones, pone*, etc. It can be reflexive when it means putting on clothes. Watch out for *salir*, too – the first person is *salgo*.

Grammar — Had a go ☐ Nearly there ☐ Nailed it! ☐

Irregular verbs (present)

1 Choose the correct verb for each answer.

Example: Mis padres *decimos* / *(dicen)* que hablo demasiado.

(a) Yo no *tiene* / *tengo* la mochila. ¿La *tienes* / *tenéis* tú?

(b) Paula le *dan* / *da* flores a nuestra madre y yo le *damos* / *doy* caramelos.

(c) Cuando mi padre *oigo* / *oye* mi música, *salgo* / *sale* de la habitación rápidamente.

(d) Si *haces* / *hace* buen tiempo, yo no *coge* / *cojo* el autobús.

(e) Alba, cuando tú y Marcos *vienes* / *venís* a casa, siempre *traen* / *traéis* regalos.

2 Complete the sentences with the correct form of the verb.

Example: A las ocho yo salgo (salir) de casa.

(a) Sube el volumen, Carlos no .... (oír) muy bien.

(b) Nunca voy a Argentina y, por eso, no .... (conocer) Buenos Aires.

(c) Nuestros primos .... (venir) a cenar esta noche.

(d) Cuando voy a la ciudad siempre .... (coger) el tren.

(e) Cada año, mi familia y yo .... (ir) de vacaciones a España.

(f) Mis amigos han decidido sus asignaturas pero yo no .... (saber) qué hacer.

(g) Marta, ¿................................ (tener) tu móvil en tu bolsa?

(h) Si hace calor en casa, simplemente me .... (poner) una camiseta.

(i) Es el cumpleaños de Elena así que yo .... (traer) un regalo.

(j) Mis profesores .... (decir) que voy a sacar buenas notas.

3 Translate these sentences into **Spanish**.

(a) I go to Spain. ....

(b) He has two sisters. ....

(c) I hear music. ....

(d) She tells the truth. ....

(e) We catch the bus. ....

(f) They do their homework. ....

(g) You (tú) go out on Saturdays. ....

(h) I give classes. ....

(i) He brings bread. ....

(j) I put the fruit on the table. ....

Had a go ☐ Nearly there ☐ Nailed it! ☐

Grammar

Ser and *estar*

> **ser:** use for permanent things (e.g. nationality, occupation, colour, size, personality)
> **estar:** use for temporary things (e.g. illness, appearance, feelings) and location

1. Write the correct form of the verb *ser* or *estar*.

   Example: Somos ingleses y vivimos en el norte del país. (ser – nosotros)

   (a) ¿Dónde .... el banco? (estar)

   (b) Mis abuelas .... muy simpáticas. (ser)

   (c) .... de Madrid, pero trabajo en Barcelona. (ser – yo)

   (d) El vestido .... verde con flores blancas. (ser)

   (e) .... las cuatro y media de la tarde. (ser)

   (f) La cama .... al lado de la puerta. (estar)

   (g) .... muy tristes hoy porque las vacaciones han terminado. (estar – vosotros)

   (h) .... listos para el examen de historia. (estar – nosotros)

2. Now translate the sentences from exercise 1 into **English**. In brackets, write down the reason why the verb is **ser** or **estar**.

   Example: We are English and we live in the north of the country. (ser for nationalities)

   (a) ....
   (b) ....
   (c) ....
   (d) ....
   (e) ....
   (f) ....
   (g) ....
   (h) ....

3. Tick the phrases which use the correct verb 'to be'. Correct those which are wrong.

   Example: Estoy en España de vacaciones. ✓
   La plaza es a la izquierda. ✗ La plaza está a la izquierda.

   (a) Somos británicos y hablamos inglés.
   ....

   (b) Mi amigo está alto y tiene el pelo negro.
   ....

   (c) Me duele la cabeza y soy enfermo.
   ....

   (d) Mi perro ha muerto y estoy muy triste.
   ....

   (e) Su primo es italiano y trabaja como profesor.
   ....

   (f) Mi madre está médica y mi padre está ingeniero.
   ....

Grammar

Had a go ☐ Nearly there ☐ Nailed it! ☐

The gerund / present participle

> Gerunds are –ing words (playing, singing, etc.). To form them replace the infinitive endings as follows:
> hablar – hablando, comer – comiendo, vivir – viviendo.
> Remember! Some verbs have irregular gerunds:
> caer → cayendo   oír → oyendo   leer → leyendo
> Some radical-changing -ir verbs also change their stem in the gerund:
> pedir → pidiendo   vestir → vistiendo

1 Change the following infinitives into the gerund, and write their meanings in **English**.

Example: beber → bebiendo – drinking

(a) comer → ....
(b) estudiar → ....
(c) correr → ....
(d) tomar → ....
(e) decir → ....
(f) recibir → ....
(g) escribir → ....
(h) escuchar → ....
(i) aprender → ....
(j) ver → ....

2 What are these people doing? Write sentences using the words from the box.

> comer paella   correr en la calle   bailar el flamenco
> hablar con amigos   escuchar música   ver una película
> navegar por Internet   escribir una carta   ~~montar en bicicleta~~

Example: (she) Está montando en bicicleta.

(a) (I) ....
(b) (they) ....
(c) (we) ....
(d) (you singular) ....

> The imperfect continuous is formed using the imperfect tense of **estar** + the gerund:
> estaba comiendo – I was eating
> **estar** in the imperfect tense: estaba, estabas, estaba, estábamos, estabais, estaban

3 Translate the first part of the sentences into **Spanish**.

Example: (I was going for a walk) Estaba dando un paseo cuando me caí al agua.

(a) (they were eating) .... cuando su madre les llamó.
(b) (we were sunbathing) .... cuando empezó a llover.
(c) (you were singing) .... cuando salió el tren.
(d) (I was playing video games) .... cuando llamó.
(e) (you all were listening to the teacher) .... cuando entró la directora.
(f) (He was studying in the library) .... cuando oyó el ruido.

Had a go ☐ Nearly there ☐ Nailed it! ☐   **Grammar**

The preterite tense

> The preterite tense is used to describe completed actions in the past. Replace the infinitive ending with:
> **–ar** verbs: é, aste, ó, amos, asteis, aron
> **–er** and **–ir** verbs: í, iste, ió, imos, isteis, ieron
> Remember! There are lots of irregular verbs in the preterite.
> At Foundation you need to learn the irregular preterite tense of the verbs: ser, ir, hacer, dar, decir, estar, poder, poner, querer, tener, traer and venir.
> At Higher tier, you also need to know those verbs that have irregular spellings in the 3rd person singular and plural, such as pidió / pidieron, sintió / sintieron, leyó / leyeron.
> At Higher tier, you should also be aware of the 1st person singular changes in -car, -zar and -gar verbs (for example saqué, empecé and llegué).

1 Write the verb in the correct form of the preterite tense.

   Example: comer (tú) → *comiste*

   (a) sacar (ellos) → ....
   (b) volver (nosotros) → ....
   (c) comprar (él) → ....
   (d) llegar (tú) → ....
   (e) trabajar (vosotros) → ....
   (f) ir (usted) → ....
   (g) dar (yo) → ....
   (h) tener (nosotros) → ....
   (i) pedir (ellas) → ....
   (j) leer (él) → ....

2 Complete the sentences with the verb in the correct form of the preterite. All these sentences use irregular verbs.

   (a) La semana pasada .... (ir) a casa de mis amigos.
   (b) Mi novio y yo no .... (tener) tiempo para visitar el museo.
   (c) Sus padres nos .... (dar) unos regalos bonitos.
   (d) Carmen .... (ir) a la playa con su hermano.
   (e) El camarero me .... (dar) un café y yo .... (pagar) en seguida.
   (f) El invierno pasado mis padres .... (ir) de vacaciones solos.
   (g) 'No es verdad', ... (decir) el niño.
   (h) El concierto .... (ser) excelente. Me gustó mucho.
   (i) .... (hacer) mis deberes antes de jugar al fútbol.
   (j) Anoche .... (tener) que lavar el coche y luego salí con mis amigos.

3 Read the text in the present tense and rewrite the text, changing all the verbs in bold into the preterite.

   Voy al cine con mis amigos y **vemos** una película de acción. Después **comemos** en un restaurante. **Como** una hamburguesa con ensalada, y mi amiga Lola **come** pollo con patatas fritas. **Bebemos** agua y mi amigo Juan toma una naranja pero yo tomo un café. Después del restaurante **voy** en tren a casa de mi prima. El viaje **es** largo y aburrido. **Vuelvo** a casa y **me acuesto** a las once de la noche.

   Fui al cine con mis amigos

   ....
   ....
   ....
   ....

Grammar

Had a go ☐ Nearly there ☐ Nailed it! ☐

The imperfect tense

> Remember! The imperfect is used:
> - to describe repeated actions in the past
> - when you would say 'used to' in English
> - to describe background details.
>
> Replace the infinitive ending with:
>
> **–ar** verbs: *aba, abas, aba, ábamos, abais, aban*
>
> **–er** and **–ir** verbs: *ía, ías, ía, íamos, íais, ían*
>
> At Foundation tier, you only need to know the first three (singular) forms of the verb in the imperfect tense.

1. Tick the sentences which contain imperfect verbs and underline the verbs.

   Example: Antes mi colegio <u>era</u> más pequeño. ✓

   (a) El miércoles fuimos a la piscina y nadamos durante una hora y media.

   (b) De pequeños nadábamos en el mar todas las semanas.

   (c) Había mucha gente en el museo y los cuadros eran muy bonitos.

   (d) Mi padre nos preparó una cena vegetariana.

   (e) Cuando eran más jóvenes, no comían ni fruta ni verdura.

   (f) Gabriela llegó a Madrid en tren para empezar su nuevo trabajo.

   (g) Ayer nos encontramos en el café y hablamos toda la tarde.

   (h) Estaba nervioso cada vez que hacía una prueba de matemáticas.

   (i) Lo pasé genial porque hizo sol y no llovió.

   (j) Nevaba todos los días y hacía un frío horrible.

2. Translate the sentences from exercise 1 into **English**. Explain your choice of tense in brackets. Write your answers on a separate piece of paper.

   Example: My school used to be smaller. (imperfect for 'used to')

3. Complete the sentences with the correct verb in the past tense. It could be either the preterite or the imperfect.

   Example: El sábado *fuimos* a la discoteca a bailar y a divertirnos. (ir)

   (a) Cuando mi hermana .... tres años empezó a tocar el piano. (tener)

   (b) Mi familia .... en el campo, pero ahora tiene un piso en Barcelona. (vivir)

   (c) .... lloviendo cuando llegamos al camping. (estar)

   (d) La semana pasada .... el coche y limpié la cocina. (lavar)

   (e) Todos los días .... en el jardín y cuidaban las flores. (trabajar)

   (f) Hizo compras por Internet y .... mucho dinero. (gastar)

   (g) Siempre .... fruta y bebíamos mucha agua para estar en forma. (comer)

   (h) Una vez .... al tenis con mi profesor de inglés, pero no gané. (jugar)

Had a go ☐ Nearly there ☐ Nailed it! ☐

Grammar

The future tense

> The **immediate future** tense is used to say what's going to happen. It is formed using the present tense of **ir** + **a** + an infinitive: *Voy a salir a las dos.* I'm going to go out at 2.
> Present tense of **ir**: *voy, vas, va, vamos, vais, van*

1 Complete the sentences with the missing parts of the immediate future tense.

   Example: I am going to buy a dress. Voy *a* comprar un vestido.

   (a) We are going to play basketball. Vamos a .... al baloncesto.

   (b) He is going to sunbathe. .... a tomar el sol.

   (c) They are going to eat fish and chips. Van .... comer pescado y patatas fritas.

   (d) I am not going to cry. No .... a llorar.

   (e) Are you going to watch the film? ¿............... a ver la película?

   (f) You (all) are going to listen and repeat. .... a escuchar y a repetir.

   (g) My mother is going to catch the bus. Mi madre .... a coger el autobús.

   (h) My friends are going to go to the UK. Mis amigos van a .... al Reino Unido.

   (i) We are not going to work on Saturdays. No .... a trabajar los sábados.

   (j) I am going to go out with my girlfriend. .... a salir con mi novia.

> The **future tense** is used to talk about what you will do or what will happen in the future. The future tense is formed by adding these endings onto the infinitive:
> *-é, -ás, -á, -emos, -éis, -án*
> Don't forget the accents!
> Remember there are some irregular future verbs: *saldré, diré, tendré, haré, podré, pondré, querré, sabré, vendré.*
> At Foundation tier, you only need to know the first three (singular) forms of the verb in the future tense.

2 Write the Spanish for these future sentences. Remember to use the future tense when describing what will happen.

   Example: I will buy a dress. *Compraré un vestido.*

   (a) We are going to watch the film. ....

   (b) I will not work on Mondays. ....

   (c) They are going to catch the underground. ....

   (d) He will go to South America. ....

   (e) They are going to play with my brother. ....

   (f) You will go to Spain. ....

3 Complete the text with the correct verbs in the immediate future tense.

   (pasar   ser   ir   visitar   ir   viajar   probar   vivir)

   El año próximo mi amiga (a) .... a la universidad a estudiar matemáticas. Yo no (b) .... a la universidad porque (c) .... seis meses trabajando para ganar experiencia. Durante este tiempo (d) .... con mis padres para ahorrar dinero. Después, (e) .... por España con mi amiga, Elena. Juntas, (f) .... todos los sitios de interés y (g) .... toda la comida especial de cada región. ¡(h) .... muy divertido!

Grammar

Had a go ☐ Nearly there ☐ Nailed it! ☐

The conditional tense

> The conditional is used to describe what you would do or what would happen in the future. To form the conditional, add the following endings to the infinitive:
>
> *ía, ías, ía, íamos, íais, ían*
>
> There are a few verbs with irregular stems and these are the same as in the future tense.
>
> At Foundation tier, you only need to know the first three (singular) forms of the verb in the conditional tense.

1 Change these future verbs into the conditional. Write the English for each.

Example: haré → *haría – I would do*

(a) compraremos → ....
(b) saldrán → ....
(c) trabajaréis → ....
(d) estará → ....
(e) jugarás → ....
(f) vendremos → ....
(g) podrás → ....
(h) habrá → ....

2 In an ideal world what would happen next year? Create sentences using the conditional.

Example: Mi madre *compraría* un perro.

(a) Mi profesor .... de vacaciones.
(b) Nuestros primos .... el sol en la playa.
(c) El jefe no .... todos los días.
(d) Mis amigos y yo .... mucho dinero.
(e) No .... contaminación del aire.
(f) Más gente .... el transporte público.
(g) Nadie .... hambre.
(h) Los gobiernos .... contra el cambio climático.
(i) Mi equipo de fútbol .... la copa.
(j) Mi hermano y yo no .... el dormitorio.

tener
ir
ganar
haber
compartir
~~comprar~~
trabajar
usar
luchar
tomar
ganar

3 Give advice using the conditional of *deber* or *poder* to help these people.

Example: Tengo dolor de cabeza. – *Deberías / Podrías dormirte un poco.*

(a) No puedo dormir.
....
(b) Como demasiados caramelos.
....
(c) No tengo energía.
....
(d) Estoy enfermo.
....
(e) Estoy cansado todo el tiempo. ....
(f) Me duelen los dientes. ....
(g) Quiero reducir la contaminación. ....
(h) Debo gastar menos dinero. ....

~~dormirte un poco~~
acostarte temprano
comer más frutas y verduras
comprar ropa de segunda mano
usar menos energía
ir al médico
ir al dentista
hacer más ejercicio
leer para descansar

Had a go ☐ Nearly there ☐ Nailed it! ☐   **Grammar**

The perfect tense

> The perfect tense is used to talk about what someone **has done** or what **has happened**.
> It is formed by taking the present tense of *haber* + a past participle.
> To form the past participle, replace the infinitive ending with:
> *-ar* verbs: *-ado*
> *-er* and *-ir* verbs: *-ido*

1 Complete the table with the correct parts of the verb *haber* and the past participle endings:

	haber (in present tense) (I have … etc)	+ past participles (spoken, eaten, lived, etc)
yo	he	
tú		habl …
él / ella / usted		com …
nosotros / nosotras	hemos	viv …
vosotros / vosotras		
ellos / ellas / ustedes		

2 Unscramble the anagrams of irregular past participles in the 3rd column and write the correct version in the 2nd column next to its infinitive.

Infinitive	Irregular past participle	Scrambled version
hacer		beatiro
volver		cheoh
abrir		cidoh
romper		lutove
ver		sotupe
escribir		tisvo
poner		toro
decir		triseco

3 Translate sentences (a) to (e) into **English** and (f) to (j) into **Spanish**.

Example: *He hablado con él.* I have spoken to him.

(a) Hemos perdido el coche. ....

(b) ¿Has estudiado español? ....

(c) Han comprado un ordenador. ....

(d) He hecho mis deberes. ....

(e) Hemos visto un programa muy informativo. ....

(f) I have broken my arm. ....

(g) They have lost their suitcase. ....

(h) We have eaten lots of sweets. ....

(i) Have you visited the museum today? ....

(j) The teachers have opened the windows. ....

Grammar

Had a go ☐ Nearly there ☐ Nailed it! ☐

Giving instructions

To give commands:
– to one person (**tú**): use the 'you' singular form of the present tense, minus the final **s**:
¡Escucha! Listen! ¡Abre! Open!
– to more than one person (**vosotros**): change the final **r** of the infinitive to **d**:
¡Escuchad! Listen! ¡Abrid! Open!
Irregular *tú* commands include:

	decir	hacer	ir	ser	poner	salir	tener	venir
tú	di	haz	ve	sé	pon	sal	ten	ven
English	say	make / do	go	be	put	leave	have	come

1. Change the following infinitives into familiar singular commands (*tú*). Be careful: some are irregular in command form.

    Example: Hablar más ⟶ Habla más.

    (a) Subir a la derecha ⟶ ....
    (b) Cruzar la plaza ⟶ ....
    (c) Pasar el puente ⟶ ....
    (d) Tener cuidado ⟶ ....
    (e) Venir aquí ⟶ ....
    (f) Cantar más bajo ⟶ ....
    (g) Leer en voz alta ⟶ ....
    (h) Escuchar bien ⟶ ....
    (i) Beber agua ⟶ ....
    (j) Hacer este ejercicio ⟶ ....

2. Now change the above commands into familiar plural ones (*vosotros*). Remember, to form the *vosotros* commands, you change the *r* of the infinitive to *d*.

    Example: Habla más. ⟶ Hablad más.

    (a) ....
    (b) ....
    (c) ....
    (d) ....
    (e) ....
    (f) ....
    (g) ....
    (h) ....
    (i) ....
    (j) ....

3. Translate these sentences into **Spanish**.

tú commands	*vosotros* / *as* commands
(a) Download the music.	(a) Buy the vegetables on the market.
(b) Make the bed.	(b) Choose your bedrooms.
(c) Visit the museum.	(c) Discuss the problem first.
(d) Sing with the music.	(d) Recycle those bottles.
(e) Leave before six.	(e) Run in the park not in the street.
(f) Always tell the truth.	(f) Clean the car on Sunday.

Had a go ☐ Nearly there ☐ Nailed it! ☐

Grammar

The present subjunctive

The subjunctive is used in a range of contexts, such as:
- after *cuando* when the action of the verb has not yet taken place: *Cuando sea mayor, voy a viajar a Bolivia.* When I am older I'm going to travel to Bolivia.
- after *para que* (so that ...): *Te mandaré la carta hoy para que la tengas antes del lunes.* I'll send you the letter today so that you have it before Monday.
- after verbs of wishing, commanding, requesting + *que*: *Quiero que vayas a pedir ayuda.* I want you to go and ask for help.
- after verbs of emotion + *que*: *Estoy muy contenta de que vengas a la fiesta.* I am very glad that you are coming to the party.

These are the five verbs that you need to know in the singular forms:
hacer (*haga, hagas*), *ser* (*sea, seas*), *venir* (*venga, vengas*), *tener* (*tenga, tengas*), *ir* (*vaya, vayas*)
The third person singular is the same as the first person singular.

1 Change these verbs from the present tense to the present subjunctive:

(a) hace → ....
(b) tienes → ....
(c) vengo → ....
(d) es → ....
(e) vas → ....
(f) tengo → ....
(g) soy → ....
(h) va → ....
(i) hago → ....
(j) vienes → ....

2 Complete the sentences with the verb in the correct form of the present subjunctive.

Example: Cuando ...*vayas*............... a la cama, apaga la luz. (ir)

(a) Cuando .... a dar un paseo, ponte gafas de sol porque hace mucho sol. (ir)

(b) Te daré mi móvil para que .... una foto. (hacer)

(c) Me sorprende que .... inglesa; pensé que eras española. (ser)

(d) Mis abuelos prefieren que yo .... en marzo este año. (venir)

(e) Mi marido quiere que .... una fiesta para mi cumpleaños. (hacer)

(f) Cuando .... diecinueve años, te permitiré viajar por España en tren. (tener)

3 Translate the sentences into **Spanish**.

(a) My sister wants me to make the evening meal.

....

(b) It annoys me that you do not come with me.

....

(c) I hope that you are lucky with the exams.

....

(d) When you go to Spain you must visit Barcelona.

....

(e) You can go to South America when you are older.

....

Grammar

Had a go ☐ Nearly there ☐ Nailed it! ☐

Negatives

> To make a sentence negative, use **no** in front of the whole verb:
>
> No me gusta la música clásica.   I don't like classical music.
> No vamos a visitar el palacio.   We are not going to visit the palace.

1 Write these sentences in the negative.

   Example: Tengo clase hoy a las diez. → No tengo clase hoy a las diez.

   (a) Estudio geografía. → ....
   (b) Vamos a la ciudad. → ....
   (c) Ricardo compró una bicicleta nueva. → ....
   (d) Sus padres vieron la tele. → ....
   (e) Voy a ir a España la semana próxima. → ....

2 Match the English and Spanish phrases. (Numbers 5–8 are Higher level phrases.)

   1 no ... nada   A never
   2 no ... nadie   B no / not any
   3 nunca   C not ... either
   4 no ... ningún / ninguna   D not ... or
   5 ya no   E no one / nobody
   6 no ... tampoco   F neither ... nor
   7 no ... ni   G not ... any more
   8 ni ... ni   H nothing / not ... anything

3 Rewrite the sentences with the negative words.

   Example: Marta habla de sus problemas. (nunca) → Marta nunca habla de sus problemas.

   > Note that *ninguno* must agree with the noun it precedes: *ninguna palabra* (no word)

   (a) Como durante el descanso. (no, nada) ....
   (b) En mi familia tuvimos un perro. (nunca) ....
   (c) Aquí tengo vestidos, faldas y camisetas. (no, ni, ni, ni) ....
   (d) Vas a comprar un coche. (no, ningún) ....
   (e) Mis padres escuchan. (no, a nadie) ....

4 Translate the sentences into **Spanish**. Be careful with the word order.

   Example: He never plays football when it rains. → Nunca juega al fútbol cuando llueve.

   (a) In the afternoon we never drink coffee. ....
   (b) I don't sing, dance or play any musical instruments. ....
   (c) They do not speak any languages. ....
   (d) We can't talk to anybody during the exam. ....
   ....
   (e) I will never smoke because it is bad for your health. ....
   ....

Had a go ☐ Nearly there ☐ Nailed it! ☐   **Grammar**

Special verbs

> A few verbs like **gustar** are used in the 3rd person with a pronoun: *Me gusta bailar.* I like dancing.
> If the thing that is liked is plural, you use **me gustan**: *Me gustan los perros.* I like dogs.
> *encantar, doler, interesar* and *importar* behave in the same way:
> *Le duele la cabeza.* His head hurts.
> *No me importa lavar los platos.* I don't mind washing the dishes.
> *¿Te interesa la historia?* Are you interested in history?

1 Complete the table with the correct pronouns.

me	gusta (sing)	I like		gusta (sing)	we like
	gustan (plu)	you like		gustan (plu)	you (all) like
		he / she / it likes			they like

> Remember! If the impersonal verb is followed by an infinitive, the singular form is used:
> *Le gusta cocinar.* He likes cooking.
> When the subject is a noun or a proper noun, you need to use *a*:
> *A Luisa le gusta salir a correr.* Luisa likes going for a run.

2 Complete the sentences.

Example: No me importa abrir la ventana. *(importar, I)*

(a) .... ir al mercado los martes. *(gustar, Paula)*

(b) ¿... las tapas en este restaurante? *(gustar, you singular)*

(c) .... visitar el castillo algún día. *(interesar, we)*

(d) .... la cabeza. *(doler, Manuel)*

(e) .... jugar juegos con la videoconsola. *(encantar, he)*

(f) No .... el calor. *(importar, I)*

(g) ¿... los pies? *(doler, you singular)*

(h) No .... mucho los programas de telerrealidad. *(interesar, I)*

> Remember!
> *acabar* (in the present tense) + *de* + infinitive ⟶ to have just … .
> *llevar* (in the present tense) + time + gerund / present participle ⟶ has / have been … ing for + time

3 Translate the sentences into **Spanish**.

(a) I have just seen a really good film.

....

(b) She has been working in the garden for two hours.

....

(c) Nadia has just finished her university course.

....

(d) We have been living here for a month.

....

(e) Your grandparents have just gone out.

....

Grammar — Had a go ☐ Nearly there ☐ Nailed it! ☐

Por and *para*

> Remember that *por* and *para* don't just mean 'for'. They can be translated in various ways depending on the sentence. For example: in, in order to, per, instead of, etc

1. Translate these sentences, which use *para*, into **English**.

    (a) Para mi cumpleaños quiero un móvil nuevo.

    ....

    (b) Mi amiga trabaja para una empresa internacional.

    ....

    (c) Las apps para iPhone son increíbles.

    ....

    (d) Como muchas verduras y pescado para estar en forma.

    ....

    (e) Necesitas arroz para hacer una paella.

    ....

    (f) Fumar es muy malo para la salud.

    ....

2. Rewrite the sentences with the word *por* in the correct place.

    Example: Muchas gracias los pantalones. *Muchas gracias por los pantalones.*

    (a) El coche rojo pasó las calles antiguas.

    ....

    (b) Normalmente la mañana me gusta tomar huevos con pan.

    ....

    (c) Mandé la información correo electrónico.

    ....

    (d) Me gustaría cambiar este vestido otro.

    ....

3. Complete the sentence with either *por* or *para*.

    Example: *Por* la tarde prefiero descansar.

    (a) .... mantener la salud, lo más importante es beber mucha agua.

    (b) Mis amigas compraron unas flores .... la profesora.

    (c) Tengo que cambiar este libro .... otro.

    (d) Hemos reservado una habitación .... tres noches.

    (e) Los alumnos tienen que terminar los ejercicios .... el lunes.

Had a go ☐ Nearly there ☐ Nailed it! ☐   **Grammar**

Asking questions

> Don't forget that Spanish question words have accents. They also have an inverted question mark (¿) at the beginning, as well as a non inverted one at the end.

1. Use the question words in the box to complete the table below.

> ~~¿Qué?~~   ¿Cuánto?   ¿Dónde?   ¿Cuándo?   ¿Cuáles?
> ¿Adónde?   ¿Por qué?   ¿Cuántos?   ¿Cómo?   ~~¿Cuál?~~

Why?	
What?	¿Qué?
When?	
How?	
Where?	
Where to?	
Which?	¿Cuál?
Which ones?	
How much?	
How many?	

2. Complete the sentences with the correct question word.
    (a) ¿............................ vive Mario?
    (b) ¿............................ vais a llegar, chicos?
    (c) ¿............................ de estas gafas son mías?
    (d) ¿............................ dinero voy a necesitar para las vacaciones?
    (e) ¿ .... piensas de la nueva profesora?
    (f) ¿............................ vamos a viajar? ¿En metro o en autobús?
    (g) ¿............................ vas a llevar a tus amigos cuando vengan?
    (h) ¿............................ personas había en el estadio para el partido?

3. Now translate the sentences in exercise 2 into **English**.

4. Match the correct answer to the question.

1	¿Por qué te pones ese traje?	A	En la cocina, sobre la mesa.
2	¿Qué compraste en el mercado?	B	Es el próximo lunes.
3	¿Dónde encontraste mi móvil?	C	Esos, los más grandes, por favor.
4	¿Cómo se comportó esta semana?	D	Porque tengo una entrevista hoy.
5	¿Cuándo tenemos el examen?	E	Unos veinte. No está muy lejos.
6	¿Cuáles quieres?	F	No voy a tardar más de diez minutos.
7	¿A cuántos kilómetros está?	G	Solo fruta y verduras.
8	¿Cuánto tiempo necesitas para terminar?	H	Muy bien. Ningún problema.

Grammar

Had a go ☐ Nearly there ☐ Nailed it! ☐

The passive (H)

> Remember that the passive can be formed in two ways. Firstly, like the English, you can use the verb *ser* (in the appropriate tense) followed by the past participle. Don't forget to make the past participle agree with the noun it refers to: **La cantante** fue acompañad**a** por la orquesta. 'The singer was accompanied by the orchestra.'

1 Complete the sentences with the correct form of the verb *ser* and the past participle. Be careful: you will need various tenses of *ser* – time phrases will indicate whether the verb took place in the past or is a present or future event.

   (a) La novela .... el siglo pasado. (escribir)

   (b) Los pisos .... el año próximo. (construir)

   (c) El centro deportivo .... por miles de personas cada semana. (usar)

   (d) Las instalaciones .... todos los días. (limpiar)

   (e) Esta mañana los estudiantes .... a la directora. (presentar)

   (f) Anoche la actriz .... varias veces en el restaurante. (reconocer)

2 Translate the sentences in exercise 1 into **English**.

   (a) ....
   (b) ....
   (c) ....
   (d) ....
   (e) ....
   (f) ....

> The other way to form the passive is to make the verb reflexive. The verb will usually be third person singular (for 'it') or third person plural for 'they'.
>
> *No se admiten perros.* 'Dogs (they) are not allowed.' ⟶ plural verb needed.
>
> *Se sirve el desayuno entre las siete y las nueve.* 'Breakfast (it) is served between 7 and 9.' ⟶ singular verb needed.

3 Complete the sentences with the correct tense in the reflexive form of the passive.

   Future

   (a) .... los resultados el lunes próximo. (publicar)

   (b) .... las cartas a todos los estudiantes. (mandar)

   Present

   (c) La película .... en una novela clásica. (basar)

   (d) .... una fiesta para los niños cada año. (organizar)

   Preterite

   (e) .... la habitación a las diez ayer. (limpiar)

   (f) .... varios móviles y portátiles de la tienda. (robar)

Had a go ☐ Nearly there ☐ Nailed it! ☐   **Grammar**

Numbers

1 Write the number.

Example: trece 13

(a) veinte ....
(b) cuarenta y ocho ....
(c) nueve ....
(d) cien ....
(e) catorce ....
(f) mil ....
(g) trescientos ....
(h) cincuenta y siete ....
(i) veintitrés ....
(j) quince ....
(k) diecinueve ....
(l) quinientos ....
(m) un millón ....
(n) novecientos ....
(o) ochenta y ocho ....
(p) setenta y seis ....
(q) sesenta y siete ....
(r) diez ....
(s) cero ....
(t) veintinueve ....

> Ordinal numbers (*primero*, *segundo*, *tercero*, etc.) are not used for dates, except for *primero* which can be used. Both of these are correct:
> *el uno de diciembre*   *el primero de diciembre*

2 Write these dates and years in **Spanish**.

Example: 4 May *el cuatro de mayo*

(a) 1999 ....
(b) 10 October ....
(c) 1 January ....
(d) 3 March ....
(e) 2013 ....
(f) 16 November ....
(g) 30 May ....
(h) 1968 ....
(i) 2002 ....
(j) 21 April ....

> To give the time, use *son las* + the number for the hour, except for 'one o'clock', which is *Es la una*.
>   *Son las ocho.* It's eight o'clock.
> For times **past** the hour, add *y cinco, y diez* etc: *Son las nueve y veinte.*
> For times **to** the hour, add *menos veinte, menos diez* etc: *Son las tres menos diez.*
>   a quarter past = *y cuarto*
>   a quarter to = *menos cuarto*
>   half past = *y media*

3 Write these times in **Spanish**.

Example: It's 5.25. *Son las cinco y veinticinco*

(a) It's 7.15 ....
(b) It's 1.25 ....
(c) It's 8.35 ....
(d) It's 11.10 ....
(e) It's 3.45 ....
(f) It's 9.50 ....
(g) It's 5.30 ....
(h) It's 12.00 ....

Paper 1: Listening (Foundation)

AQA publishes official Sample Assessment Material on its website. This test has been written to help you practise what you have learned across the four skills and may not be representative of a real exam paper.

Technology

Track 104

1 Luis, Julia and Antonio are talking about technology. What do they say? Write the correct letter in each box.

1.1 In the afternoons, Luis …

A	looks at social media.
B	plays computer games.
C	does a computer course.

(1 mark)

1.2 Julia is buying a new …

A	mobile.
B	laptop.
C	app.

(1 mark)

1.3 Antonio thinks it is useful …

A	to text his friends.
B	to send emails.
C	to shop online.

(1 mark)

Hotel accommodation

Track 105

2 Manuel is talking about a hotel he stayed in. What **three** aspects of the hotel does he mention? Write the correct letters in the boxes.

A	restaurant	D	gardens
B	bedroom	E	games room
C	swimming pool	F	views

(3 marks)

Transport

Track 106

3 Pilar is talking in a podcast. What does she say about transport in her area? Complete the sentences. Write the correct letter in each box.

3.1 Pilar goes into town …

A	by car.
B	on the train.
C	on her bike.

(1 mark)

3.2 Pilar gets around town …

A	on the underground.
B	on foot.
C	on the bus.

(1 mark)

3.3 She thinks cycling in town is …

A	fun.
B	easy.
C	dangerous.

(1 mark)

Had a go ☐ **Nearly there** ☐ **Nailed it!** ☐ **Practice papers**

School

Track 107

4 Daniela is talking to her mother about getting a new uniform. What **three** things does she say she needs? Write the correct letters in the boxes.

A	dress	C	shoes	E	trousers
B	shirt	D	skirt	F	T-shirt

☐ ☐ ☐   **(3 marks)**

Free-time activities

Track 108

5 Diego is talking about what he is doing this evening. What does he say?

Complete the sentences in **English**.

5.1 Diego is going to see the latest film by his ……………………………… . **(1 mark)**

5.2 It is a ……………………………………………………………… film. **(1 mark)**

5.3 They say the ……………………………………………… will win a prize. **(1 mark)**

5.4 He thinks going to the cinema is ……………………………………………… . **(1 mark)**

TV preferences

Track 109

6 Alba is talking about what she likes on TV. What does she say? Write the correct letter in each box.

6.1 Her favourite series is …

A	a cooking competition.
B	a painting programme.
C	a dance show.

☐ **(1 mark)**

6.2 She thinks the people that do best in the series are …

A	singers.
B	actors.
C	sportspeople.

☐ **(1 mark)**

6.3 The winners are generally … .

A	women.
B	older people.
C	young.

☐ **(1 mark)**

Sports

Track 110

7 David is talking about his favourite football player. What does he say? Write the correct answer in each box.

7.1 The footballer currently plays …

A	for an Argentinian team.
B	in Spain.
C	for his country.

☐ **(1 mark)**

7.2 The player …

A	trains hard with the team.
B	is well respected by his followers.
C	is fast and very fit.

☐ **(1 mark)**

7.3 In the last match, he …

A	was injured.
B	scored the winning goal.
C	could not play as he was ill.

☐ **(1 mark)**

Practice papers

Had a go ☐ Nearly there ☐ Nailed it! ☐

Track 111

Eating out

Miguel is talking about eating out when on holiday.

Write the correct **number** of the food that Miguel describes. Write the correct **letter** for when he tries it.

Food			When	
1	Fish dish	P	Past
2	Meat dish	N	Now
3	Vegetarian dish	F	Future
4	Dessert		

Food   When

8 ☐ ☐ **(2 marks)**

9 ☐ ☐ **(2 marks)**

Track 112

A healthy lifestyle

10 Ana, Fernando and Lucía are talking about their lifestyle. Which aspect is each person talking about? Write the correct letter in each box.

A	A new hobby	C	Drinking more water	E	Going to the gym
B	Avoiding fatty foods	D	Getting fitter	F	Using less technology

10.1 Ana ☐ **(1 mark)**

10.2 Fernando ☐ **(1 mark)**

10.3 Lucía ☐ **(1 mark)**

Track 113

Life at school

Marta, Carlos and Álex are talking about events at school. What is their opinion of the things they talk about?

Write **P** for a positive opinion

N for a negative opinion

P+N for a positive and negative opinion.

11 Marta ☐ **(1 mark)**

12 Carlos ☐ **(1 mark)**

13 Álex ☐ **(1 mark)**

Dictation

Track 114

You will now hear four short sentences. Listen carefully and using your knowledge of Spanish sounds, write down in **Spanish** exactly what you hear for each sentence.

You will hear each sentence **three** times: the first time as a full sentence, the second time in short sections and the third time again as a full sentence.

Sentence 1 ....

Sentence 2 ....

Sentence 3 ....

Sentence 4 ....

(8 marks)

TOTAL FOR PAPER = 40 MARKS

Had a go ☐ Nearly there ☐ Nailed it! ☐   **Practice papers**

Paper 2: Speaking (Foundation)

Role play

1. You are talking to your Chilean friend. Listen to the recording of the teacher's part. The teacher will play the part of your friend and will speak first.

   You should address your friend as *tú*.

   When you see this – **?** – you will have to ask a question.

   > **In order to score full marks, you must include a verb in your response to each task.**
   > 1 Say what your favourite subject is. (Give **one** detail.)
   > 2 Say what you think of your uniform. (Give **one** detail.)
   > 3 Say what you do during break at school. (Give **one** detail.)
   > 4 Say when you do your homework. (Give **one** detail.)
   > ?5 Ask your friend a question about teachers.

   (10 marks)

Reading aloud

2. Read aloud the following text in **Spanish**.

   > Me interesan mucho las redes sociales.
   > Puedes hacer juegos, seguir a la gente famosa y escuchar música.
   > Siempre tengo mi móvil.
   > Lo uso para llamar a mis amigos y compañeros.
   > También veo películas a veces.

   Then listen to the recording of four questions in **Spanish** that relate to the topic of **Media and technology**. In order to score the highest marks, you must try to **answer all four questions as fully as you can**. **(15 marks)**

Photo card

3. Look at the two photos as part of your preparation. Make as many notes as you want on an Additional Answer Sheet for use during the test. You will be asked about the content of these photos by your teacher. The recommended time is approximately **one minute. You must say at least one thing about each photo.** After you have spoken about the content of the photos, you will then be asked questions related to **any** of the topics within the theme of **Popular culture**.

   (25 marks)

Photo 1

Photo 2

TOTAL FOR PAPER = 50 MARKS

Paper 3: Reading (Foundation)

SECTION A

Caring for the environment

Read these comments from an internet forum.

> **Ana:** Normalmente, me gusta ir al colegio en bicicleta. Nunca dejo mi basura cuando voy al campo.
>
> **Bruno:** Siempre voy a pie al instituto. Apago las luces en casa cuando mi hermano se olvida.
>
> **Carla:** Reciclo todas las bolsas de plástico en casa. Tengo mucho cuidado con el agua – intento no usar mucha.

Answer the following questions.

Write   **A** for Ana

   B for Bruno

   C for Carla.

Write the correct letter in each box.

1   Who turns off lights?   ☐   (1 mark)

2   Who cycles to school?   ☐   (1 mark)

3   Who recycles plastic bags?   ☐   (1 mark)

4   Who is careful with water?   ☐   (1 mark)

5   Who never drops litter?   ☐   (1 mark)

6   Who walks to school?   ☐   (1 mark)

A shopping trip

Read Sofía's text message.

> Hola
>
> Voy a la ciudad esta tarde para comprar ropa. Voy a gastar el dinero que recibí para mi cumpleaños. Iré a la tienda de ropa al lado de la estación primero, porque las cosas allí no son demasiado caras. Creo que buscaré también en el mercado porque vi unas camisetas bonitas allí en el pasado.

7   Which **three** statements are correct? Write the correct letter in each box.

   Sofía ...

A	wants to buy clothes.	D	doesn't want anything too dear.
B	is buying a birthday present.	E	says there is no market today.
C	will try the shop next to the bank.	F	is looking for a T-shirt.

☐ ☐ ☐   (3 marks)

Had a go ☐ **Nearly there** ☐ **Nailed it!** ☐

Practice papers

Sports activities

Read this programme of activities.

> Si los niños en tu familia están aburridos durante las vacaciones, aquí organizamos varias actividades para los meses de verano. Por las mañanas, hay clases de tenis. Por las tardes, tenemos concursos de baloncesto para los jóvenes, con una copa para los **ganadores**.

Complete the sentences below. Write the letter for the correct option in each box.

8 The activities are for …

A	the whole family.
B	bored children.
C	talented players.

☐ **(1 mark)**

9 They are being held …

A	through the summer months.
B	every weekend.
C	for six weeks.

☐ **(1 mark)**

10 In the afternoons you can play …

A	basketball.
B	tennis.
C	football.

☐ **(1 mark)**

11 Read the last sentence again. What are *ganadores*?

Write the correct letter in the box.

A	winners
B	referees
C	organisers

☐ **(1 mark)**

A visit to the cinema

Read Paula and Martín's comments in a blog.

> **Paula:** El año pasado vi muchas películas de ese director y normalmente son buenas. Sin embargo, su última película es muy lenta y difícil de entender.
>
> En la otra sala, hay una película que es una historia de amor. Voy a verla la semana próxima.
>
> **Martín:** En el cine las otras personas hacen mucho ruido y lo odio. Siempre están comiendo algo o hablando demasiado alto.
>
> Prefiero estar en casa porque puedo parar la película cuando quiero.

Answer the following questions in **English**.

12 What did Paula think of the director's last film? (Give **one** detail)

………………………………………………………………………………………… **(1 mark)**

13 What type of film is on the other screen?

………………………………………………………………………………………… **(1 mark)**

14 Why is it noisy in the cinema, according to Martín? (Give **one** detail)

………………………………………………………………………………………… **(1 mark)**

15 Why does Martín prefer to watch films at home?

………………………………………………………………………………………… **(1 mark)**

Practice papers

Had a go ☐ Nearly there ☐ Nailed it! ☐

Local events

Read this article from a local web page.

> El día cuatro de enero muchas de las carreteras en el centro de la ciudad estarán cerradas al tráfico por la mañana. Están preparando las calles para la fiesta del día después y el desfile a la iglesia el viernes. Si tienes que ir a la ciudad, recomendamos dejar el coche en casa.
>
> Parece que no vamos a tener buen tiempo. Entonces si tenéis frío después del desfile podéis venir a la plaza mayor para tomar un café caliente.

Which statements are correct?

Write **A** if only statement **A** is correct

     B if only statement **B** is correct

     A + B if both statements **A and B** are correct.

Write the correct letter in each box.

16 On 4th January …

A	some roads in town will be closed.
B	the town festival begins.

☐ (1 mark)

17 There is going to be a …

A	street market.
B	religious parade.

☐ (1 mark)

18 You are recommended to …

A	come into town early.
B	leave the car at home.

☐ (1 mark)

19 The article says …

A	you might feel cold.
B	hot drinks will be served.

☐ (1 mark)

School

Read David's comments about his school.

> Soy el nuevo alumno en el instituto porque solo vinimos a vivir al pueblo en junio. En general estoy contento aquí – aunque a veces me pierdo en el edificio, y eso me molesta mucho.
>
> En mi antiguo instituto, tenía problemas con las matemáticas, y aquí las clases son difíciles de seguir también. Las que más disfruto ahora son las clases de dibujo.
>
> Mi profesora favorita es una mujer inglesa que nos da clases de ciencias. Es muy divertida y nos hace sonreír mucho.

What is his opinion of these aspects of school?

Write **P** for a positive opinion

     N for a negative opinion

     P+N for a positive and negative opinion.

Write the correct letter in each box.

20 His general feelings about the new school ☐ (1 mark)

21 His experience of Maths ☐ (1 mark)

22 His art classes ☐ (1 mark)

23 The science teacher ☐ (1 mark)

My town

Read Sandra's blog about her town.

> Me encanta mi pueblo y he vivido aquí toda mi vida, pero sé que hay cosas que tenemos que cambiar. Aquí voy a hablar de los aspectos positivos y negativos del pueblo.
>
> Primero quiero dar las gracias a la gente que limpia las calles. Hacen un trabajo excelente y mantienen nuestro pueblo libre de basura.
>
> Creo que necesitamos más sitios de juego para los niños, especialmente los que viven en pisos y no tienen jardín. Hay sitio para un nuevo parque detrás del supermercado.
>
> Los autobuses que van a la ciudad son modernos y cómodos, pero solo hay dos al día. Hay mucha gente mayor que necesita más autobuses.
>
> Me **inquieta** el número de accidentes que hay en las calles cerca del instituto. Con todos los coches, es ahora una zona peligrosa.

Complete the sentences.

Write the letter for the correct option in each box.

24 Sandra's blog about the town points out …

A	the positive aspects.
B	the negative side.
C	both good and bad.

(1 mark)

25 Sandra …

A	complains about litter.
B	thinks the town is clean.
C	has been litter-picking.

(1 mark)

26 Sandra thinks they need more …

A	play areas.
B	flats.
C	gardens.

(1 mark)

27 Sandra says that the buses …

A	are old and dirty.
B	never run on time.
C	are not frequent enough.

(1 mark)

28 Read the last two sentences again. What emotion does the word **inquieta** express?

Write the correct letter in the box.

A	pleasure
B	worry
C	impatience

(1 mark)

Practice papers

Had a go ☐ Nearly there ☐ Nailed it! ☐

Advice for shoppers

Read the shopping advice in this article.

> No tienes que comprar todo del supermercado. Puedes ir al mercado al final del día porque entonces a menudo venden verduras y fruta a precios muy buenos.
>
> Recomiendo comer algo antes de ir – no debes tener hambre cuando haces la compra. Siempre mira cuánto cuestan los diferentes productos – las marcas famosas son más caras y no siempre mejores. También debes leer la información en los productos, especialmente si quieres saber los ingredientes que hay en la comida.

Complete these sentences. Write the letter for the correct option in each box.

29 At the end of the day you should shop at the …

A	market.
B	supermarket.
C	shopping centre.

☐ (1 mark)

30 When you go shopping, make sure you …

A	take your own bags.
B	are not hungry.
C	have your list.

☐ (1 mark)

31 The famous brands are not always the …

A	best.
B	most expensive.
C	healthiest.

☐ (1 mark)

32 Read the product information to find out …

A	the way to cook it.
B	how long it lasts.
C	what is in it.

☐ (1 mark)

A new sports centre

Read these social media comments about a new sports centre.

> **Julia:** Yo tengo sesenta años y nunca he aprendido a nadar. Este centro de deportes es genial porque tiene clases en la piscina para la gente mayor. El único problema es que no hay mucho sitio donde se puede dejar el coche.
>
> **Omar:** El aspecto que más me gusta es el café con vistas a la piscina. Puedo tomar un café mientras miro a mis hijos en el agua. Creo que deberían subir un poco la temperatura del agua – mis hijos dicen que está muy fría.
>
> **Carmen:** Esta semana fui a mi primera clase de baile moderno. La profesora es increíble y mis compañeros son gente muy simpática. Lo único que no me gusta es que empiezan muy temprano. Se debería comenzar una hora más tarde.

Had a go ☐   Nearly there ☐   Nailed it! ☐

Practice papers

Answer the questions in **English**.

33 What will Julia have the opportunity to do at the sports centre?

.... **(1 mark)**

34 What problem does Julia mention?

.... **(1 mark)**

35 Why does Omar like the café?

.... **(1 mark)**

36 What recommendation does Omar make?

.... **(1 mark)**

37 What does Carmen say about this week?

Write the correct letter in the box.

A	She qualified as a dance teacher.
B	She started dance lessons.
C	She had to cancel her first class.

(1 mark)

38 What is Carmen's only criticism?

Write the correct letter in the box.

A	The room is not suitable.
B	The start time is not ideal.
C	The classes end too late.

(1 mark)

SECTION B

Translation into English

39 Translate these sentences into **English**.

Quiero un trabajo durante las vacaciones de verano.

.... **(2 marks)**

Me gustaría aprender a tocar un instrumento musical.

.... **(2 marks)**

Tuvimos una fiesta después de los exámenes.

.... **(2 marks)**

Mi primo está pasando un año en el extranjero.

.... **(2 marks)**

Voy a subir estas fotos de mi móvil.

.... **(2 marks)**

TOTAL FOR PAPER = 50 MARKS

Paper 4: Writing (Foundation)

Had a go ☐ Nearly there ☐ Nailed it! ☐

In the real exam, you will write your answers on the question paper. Here, you will need to write some of the answers on your own paper.

SECTION A

1 You decide to send this photo on WhatsApp to a friend in Peru.

   What is in this photo? Write **five** sentences in **Spanish**.

   1.1 .... **(2 marks)**

   1.2 .... **(2 marks)**

   1.3 .... **(2 marks)**

   1.4 .... **(2 marks)**

   1.5 .... **(2 marks)**

2 Write an email to your Mexican friend about healthy living and lifestyle. Write approximately **50** words in **Spanish**. You must write something about each bullet point.

   Mention:
   - what you eat
   - what you do not eat
   - exercise
   - free time
   - activities with friends.

   (10 marks)

3 Using your knowledge of grammar, complete the following sentences in **Spanish**. Choose the correct Spanish word from the three options in the grid. Write the correct **word** in the space, as shown in the example below.

   Example El autobús ......*llega*...... a las ocho.

   3.1 Me .... mucho las ciencias.

   3.2 Quiero .... una revista.

   3.3 Voy al parque .... jugar al fútbol.

   3.4 Normalmente .... levanto a las siete.

   3.5 ¿.................... personas hay en tu familia?

llego	llegan	llega
gusta	gusto	gustan
compro	comprar	compra
para	por	porque
yo	me	mi
Cuántos	Cuántas	Cuánta

   (5 marks)

4 Translate the following sentences into **Spanish**.

   I do not wear glasses.

   I work in a café on Saturdays.

   We are going to study in the library.

   My dog sleeps in the kitchen.

   There was a lot of litter in the streets.

   (10 marks)

SECTION B

An article

5 Choose either Question 5(a) or Question 5(b).

(a) Write an article about home and the environment: You **must** include the following points: • what you and your friends do in your area • something you did recently to help the local environment • what your ideal home would be like.	(b) Write an article about education. You **must** include the following points: • what you think about your school • a trip that you went on with school • what you will study in the future.

   Write your answer in **Spanish**. You should aim to write approximately **90** words. **(15 marks)**

   TOTAL FOR PAPER = 50 MARKS

Had a go ☐   Nearly there ☐   Nailed it! ☐

Practice papers

Paper 1: Listening (Higher)

AQA publishes official Sample Assessment Material on its website. This test has been written to help you practise what you have learned across the four skills and may not be representative of a real exam paper.

Life at school

Marta, Carlos and Álex are talking about events at school. What is their opinion of the things they talk about?

Write **P** for a positive opinion
       N for a negative opinion
       P+N for a positive and negative opinion.

1 Marta [ ] **(1 mark)**   2 Carlos [ ] **(1 mark)**   3 Álex [ ] **(1 mark)**

Eating out

Miguel is talking about eating out when on holiday. Write the correct **number** of the food that Miguel describes. Write the correct **letter** for when he tries it.

Food	
1	Fish dish
2	Meat dish
3	Vegetarian dish
4	Dessert

When	
A	Past
B	Now
C	Future

	Food	When	
4	[ ]	[ ]	**(2 marks)**
5	[ ]	[ ]	**(2 marks)**

Holidays

Elena is talking about the town where she goes on holiday. What does she say?

Choose the correct answer and write the letter in each box.

6.1 Tourists tend to stay …

A	on the coast.
B	in apartments.
C	by their hotel pool.

[ ] **(1 mark)**

6.2 Some people never go …

A	into the countryside.
B	up to the mountains.
C	to see the old town.

[ ] **(1 mark)**

6.3 On holiday, Elena stays …

A	in a house she owns.
B	in a rented flat.
C	on a campsite.

[ ] **(1 mark)**

6.4 The adults enjoy …

A	swimming and sunbathing.
B	playing with the children.
C	reading by the pool.

[ ] **(1 mark)**

Free-time activities

Diego is talking about what he is doing this evening. What does he say?

Complete **both** the sentences in **English**.

7.1 Diego is going to see the latest film by his ………………………………………… . **(1 mark)**

7.2 It is a ………………………………………………………………… film. **(1 mark)**

Complete both parts of question 8.

8.1 They say the ………………………………………… will win a prize. **(1 mark)**

8.2 He thinks going to the cinema is ………………………………………… . **(1 mark)**

129

Practice papers

Had a go ☐ Nearly there ☐ Nailed it! ☐

Family

Track 122

Laura is talking about her family. What does she say?

Complete the sentences. Write the correct letter in each box.

9.1 Laura is unhappy at home because …

A	she does not get on with her parents.
B	the atmosphere is awful.
C	she is always fighting with her brother.

(1 mark)

9.2 Laura's father …

A	owns his own company.
B	is having trouble at work.
C	has lost his job.

(1 mark)

9.3 Laura's brother, Juan, …

A	is in trouble with the police.
B	does not intend to follow his father's wishes.
C	wants to be a film director.

(1 mark)

Relationships

Track 123

Hugo is talking about his sister, María. What does he say? Complete the sentences. Write the correct letter in each box.

10.1 Hugo's sister, María, …

A	went to a university party.
B	has just met a Cuban boy.
C	has a long-term boyfriend.

(1 mark)

10.2 Last night …

A	María came home really angry.
B	Hugo heard María crying.
C	María went out for a meal.

(1 mark)

10.3 Hugo thinks …

A	his mum argued with María.
B	María got a text that upset her.
C	María and her boyfriend broke up.

(1 mark)

Education

Track 124

Ana, Vicente and Carla are talking about the advantages and disadvantages of continuing their course of studies at school. What do they say?

Write **A** if only statement **A** is correct

   B if only statement **B** is correct

   A+B if both statements **A and B** are correct.

Write the correct letter(s) in each box.

11.1 Ana …

A	has clear plans for the future.
B	does not want to do PE.

(1 mark)

11.2 Vicente …

A	hopes to go on and get a degree.
B	is happy they will have the same teachers.

(1 mark)

11.3 Carla …

A	is glad to stay with schoolfriends.
B	wishes school was nearer home.

(1 mark)

Had a go ☐ **Nearly there** ☐ **Nailed it!** ☐   **Practice papers**

The environment

Álex is talking about his experiences last year. What does he say? Complete the sentences in English. Write one word in each space.

12.1 Last year was one of the ………………………… he has ever known. **(1 mark)**

12.2 On holiday they had one day of …………………………. **(1 mark)**

Earning money

Toni, Paula and Jaime are talking about earning money. Answer **all** parts of the question in **English**.

13 Why does Toni need money? ………………………………………………………… **(1 mark)**

14 Why does Paula not spend her money? ……………………………………………… **(1 mark)**

15 Why did Jaime's parents say he could not take the job?

Choose the correct answer and write the letter in the box.

A	Jaime is too young.
B	He would have to work too late.
C	It would affect his school work.

☐ **(1 mark)**

A festival

Susana, Pablo and Isabel are talking about the festival next week. Which aspect is each one looking forward to? Write the correct letter in each box.

A	Guided tour
B	Concert
C	Eating out
D	Market
E	Parade
F	Receiving presents

16.1 Susana ☐ **(1 mark)**   16.2 Pablo ☐ **(1 mark)**   16.3 Isabel ☐ **(1 mark)**

A project on the local area

Simón is doing a school project on his town. Write the **letter** of the topic is he going to cover and the **number** for where he will get the information.

	Topic		Information from …
A	Architecture	1	Grandparents
B	Famous people	2	Internet
C	Industry	3	Local history books
D	Nature	4	Town hall

	Topic	Information from …
17	☐	☐
18	☐	☐

(2 marks)

(2 marks)

Practice papers

Had a go ☐ Nearly there ☐ Nailed it! ☐

An interview

Lucía is interviewing a famous actor. What do they say? Complete the sentences. Write the correct letter in each box. **Answer both parts of question 19**.

19.1 Lucía asks him if he …

A	was in school plays.
B	went to the theatre as a child.
C	studied drama when younger.

☐ (1 mark)

19.2 The actor remembers …

A	his first romantic film.
B	having to learn his first lines for a play.
C	an embarrassing early role.

☐ (1 mark)

Answer both parts of question 20

20.1 Lucía asks him …

A	where he lives these days.
B	how he feels about being famous.
C	about his next role.

☐ (1 mark)

20.2 The actor …

A	is making a costume drama next.
B	gets angry with press photographers.
C	wants privacy for his family.

☐ (1 mark)

Dictation

You will now hear five short sentences. Listen carefully and using your knowledge of Spanish sounds, write down in **Spanish** exactly what you hear for each sentence. You will hear each sentence **three** times: the first time as a full sentence, the second time in short sections and the third time again as a full sentence.

Sentence 1

....

Sentence 2

....

Sentence 3

....

Sentence 4

....

Sentence 5

....

(10 marks)
TOTAL FOR PAPER = 50 MARKS

Had a go ☐ Nearly there ☐ Nailed it! ☐   **Practice papers**

Paper 2: Speaking (Higher)

Track 131

Role play

You are talking to your Argentinian friend. Play the recording of the teacher's part. The teacher will play the part of your friend and will speak first.

You should address your friend as *tú*.

When you see this – ? – you will have to ask a question.

> **In order to score full marks, you must include a verb in your response to each task.**
> 1 Say what is good about your area. (Give **two** details.)
> 2 Say what aspects of your area you do not like. (Give **two** details.)
> 3 Say what you think about the weather in your area. (Give **one** detail.)
> 4 Say where you went in your area last weekend. (Give **two** details.)
> ?5 Ask your friend a question about their town.

(10 marks)

Reading aloud

Read aloud the following text in **Spanish**.

> Mi actriz favorita es una mujer muy hermosa con el pelo largo y los ojos marrones.
> Ha sido la estrella de varias series de televisión.
> Tiene muchos seguidores en Sudamérica porque es de una familia mexicana.
> Sale en anuncios para productos de cuidado de la piel también.
> No sé cuántos años tiene.

Track 132

Then play the recording of four questions in **Spanish** that relate to the theme of **Popular culture**. In order to score the highest marks, you must try to **answer all four questions as fully as you can.**

(15 marks)

Photo card

Track 133

Look at the two photos as part of your preparation. Make as many notes as you want on an Additional Answer Sheet for use during the test. You will be asked about the content of these photos by your teacher. The recommended time is approximately **one and a half minutes. You must say at least one thing about each photo.** After you have spoken about the content of the photos, you will then be asked questions related to **any** of the topics within the theme of **People and lifestyle**.

(25 marks)

Photo 1

Photo 2

TOTAL FOR PAPER = 50 MARKS

Paper 3: Reading (Higher)

SECTION A

School

Read David's comments about his school.

> Soy el nuevo alumno en el colegio porque solo vinimos a vivir al pueblo en junio. Generalmente estoy contento aquí – aunque a veces me pierdo en el edificio, y eso me molesta mucho.
>
> En mi antiguo instituto, tenía problemas con las matemáticas, y aquí las clases son difíciles de seguir también. Las que más disfruto ahora son las clases de dibujo.
>
> Mi profesora favorita es una mujer inglesa que nos da clases de ciencias. Es muy divertida y nos hace sonreír mucho.

What is his opinion of these aspects of school?

Write **P** for a positive opinion

   N for a negative opinion

   P+N for a positive and negative opinion.

Write the correct letter in each box.

1 His general feelings about the new school ☐ **(1 mark)**

2 His experience of Maths ☐ **(1 mark)**

3 His art classes ☐ **(1 mark)**

4 The science teacher ☐ **(1 mark)**

My town

Read Sandra's blog about her town.

> Me encanta mi pueblo y he vivido aquí toda mi vida, pero sé que hay cosas que tenemos que cambiar. Aquí voy a hablar de los aspectos positivos y negativos del pueblo.
>
> Primero quiero dar las gracias a la gente que limpia las calles. Hacen un trabajo excelente y mantienen nuestro pueblo libre de basura.
>
> Creo que necesitamos más sitios de juego para los niños, especialmente los que viven en pisos y no tienen jardín. Hay sitio para un nuevo parque detrás del supermercado.
>
> Los autobuses que van a la ciudad son modernos y cómodos, pero solo hay dos al día. Hay mucha gente mayor que necesita un servicio más frecuente.
>
> Estoy muy preocupada por el número de accidentes que hay en las calles cerca del instituto. Con todos los **camiones**, es ahora una zona peligrosa.

Had a go ☐ **Nearly there** ☐ **Nailed it!** ☐   **Practice papers**

Complete the sentences. Write the correct letter in each box.

5 Sandra's blog about the town points out …

A	the positive aspects.
B	the negative side.
C	both good and bad.

☐ **(1 mark)**

6 Sandra …

A	complains about litter.
B	thinks the town is clean.
C	has been litter-picking.

☐ **(1 mark)**

7 Sandra thinks they need more …

A	play areas.
B	flats.
C	gardens.

☐ **(1 mark)**

8 Sandra says that the buses …

A	are old and dirty.
B	never run on time.
C	are not frequent enough.

☐ **(1 mark)**

9 Read the last paragraph again. What are **camiones**?

Write the correct letter in the box.

A	A type of weather
B	A type of job
C	A type of transport

☐ **(1 mark)**

Advice for shoppers

Read the shopping advice in this article.

> No tienes que comprar todo del supermercado. Puedes ir al mercado al final del día porque entonces a menudo venden verduras y fruta a precios muy buenos.
>
> Recomiendo comer algo antes de ir – no debes tener hambre cuando haces la compra. Siempre mira cuánto cuestan los diferentes productos – las marcas famosas son más caras y no siempre mejores. También debes leer la información en los productos, especialmente si quieres saber los ingredientes que hay en la comida.

Complete the sentences. Write the correct letter in each box.

10 At the end of the day you should shop at the …

A	market.
B	supermarket.
C	shopping centre.

☐ **(1 mark)**

11 When you go shopping, make sure you …

A	take your own bags.
B	are not hungry.
C	have your list.

☐ **(1 mark)**

12 The famous brands are not always the …

A	best.
B	most expensive.
C	healthiest.

☐ **(1 mark)**

13 Read the product information to find out …

A	the way to cook it.
B	how long it lasts.
C	what is in it.

☐ **(1 mark)**

Practice papers — Had a go ☐ Nearly there ☐ Nailed it! ☐

A holiday home website

Read these reviews of a holiday home website.

> **Carlos:** El sitio web es muy útil y las fotos muestran imágenes muy claras de las casas que se puede alquilar. Es un poco decepcionante que no tenga la dirección de las casas, porque siempre quiero ver exactamente dónde están.
>
> **Rosa:** Este año queremos pasar todo el verano en la costa y es difícil saber cuánto cuesta por mes. Solo dan los precios por semana. Agradecí las respuestas rápidas a mis preguntas. Contestaron normalmente en menos de un día.

What aspect was each reviewer satisfied with? What were they **not** satisfied with?

A	Contact details	C	Location information	E	Quality of photos
B	Distance to beach details	D	Price information	F	Response to emails

Write the correct letter in each box.

                Satisfied with … Not satisfied with …

14 Carlos ☐ ☐ **(2 marks)**

15 Rosa ☐ ☐ **(2 marks)**

Travel problems

Read Laura's blog about travel problems.

> Cogí el vuelo de Madrid a las Islas Canarias* para pasar unas semanas con mi tía. Le dije que iba a llegar a las diez de la mañana, pero me olvidé de que hay una diferencia de una hora entre España y allí. Saqué mi móvil para explicarle la hora de llegada correcta, pero no tenía señal. Cuando mi vuelo llegó, tuve que pasar una hora en el café esperando a mi tía. **Laura**

las Islas Canarias – The Canary Islands

16 Which statements are true about Laura's trip? Write the **three** correct letters in the boxes.

A	Laura went to her aunt's by plane.	D	She managed to text her aunt.
B	Laura said she would arrive at ten.	E	She left her phone behind.
C	She forgot there was a time difference.	F	Her aunt had to wait ages for her to arrive.

☐ ☐ ☐ **(3 marks)**

Relationships

Read this summary of the latest events in a daily TV series.

> Rodrigo se peleó con su novia, Lorena, hace una semana y tuvieron una discusión bastante seria. Rodrigo le admitió a sus amigos el día después que ya no quiere salir con ella. Pero no ha dicho nada a Lorena porque están pasando un fin de semana en un hotel de lujo – que ella pagó. El muy malo dice que romperá con ella dentro de unos días.

Had a go ☐ **Nearly there** ☐ **Nailed it!** ☐ — Practice papers

When do these events happen according to the summary?

Write **P** for something that happened **in the past**

N for something that is happening **now**

F for something that is going to happen **in the future**.

Write the correct letter in each box.

17 The argument ☐ **(1 mark)**   **19** The chat with friends ☐ **(1 mark)**

18 The break-up ☐ **(1 mark)**   **20** The hotel weekend ☐ **(1 mark)**

A nature reserve

Read this extract from the website of a nature reserve.

> En nuestro parque natural encontrarás ejemplos de muchos tipos de hábitat, desde tierra seca hasta lagos bastante grandes. Verás pájaros que descansan aquí en verano antes de continuar su viaje al norte.
>
> La gente que nos visita recomienda empezar en el centro educativo donde hay una lista de los pájaros que hemos visto en el parque esa semana. Así puedes tener una buena idea de lo que podrías ver en la reserva. En caso de mal tiempo hay juegos y actividades para los pequeños si tenéis que entrar para evitar **un chubasco**.

Write **A** if only statement **A** is correct

B if only statement **B** is correct

A + B if both statements **A and B** are correct.

Write the correct letter(s) in the boxes.

21 In the reserve …

A	there are areas of dry land.
B	there are areas of water.

(1 mark)

22 Some of the birds …

A	live there permanently.
B	are summer visitors.

(1 mark)

23 It is a good idea …

A	to start in the visitors' centre.
B	to check out the list of what to see.

(1 mark)

24 Read the last sentence again. What is **un chubasco**?

Write the correct letter in the box.

A	a type of game
B	a type of weather
C	a type of food

(1 mark)

Facilities at the nature reserve

Read the extra information on the website.

> Aunque hay una gran zona para dejar los coches, recomendamos venir en tren porque hay una estación a un cuarto de hora andando. Si muestras el billete de tren te cobramos dos euros menos para entrar.
>
> En los jardines hay mesas y sillas para comer al aire libre si traes comida de casa. O puedes disfrutar de una variedad de platos fríos y calientes servidos en nuestro restaurante.
>
> Los pequeños pueden divertirse en el parque infantil o subir a los árboles en el bosque - bajo la supervisión de sus padres (¡claro!).

Practice papers Had a go ☐ Nearly there ☐ Nailed it! ☐

What does the information tell us? Answer the following questions in **English**.

25 What is the benefit of travelling by train? .... **(1 mark)**

26 What does the restaurant provide? .... **(1 mark)**

27 What can children do in the woods? .... **(1 mark)**

My favourite novel

Read Rosalía's review of a novel.

> Leí esta novela por primera vez cuando tenía diecisiete años y, muchas veces, las opiniones cambian con el tiempo. Pero cuando la leí otra vez la semana pasada me gustó tanto como antes. Reconozco que es una novel larguísima, de unas cuatrocientas páginas, y no es una historia fácil para pasar un rato en la playa en verano. Esta novela necesita tu tiempo y dedicación, ¡pero vale la pena!
>
> El libro cuenta la historia de Alba, una chica nueva en un instituto privado que está lleno de los hijos y las hijas de gente muy rica. Ella también parece ser de una familia con dinero, pero está escondiendo un secreto. En realidad, es la hija de una de las mujeres que limpia el colegio y le han dado una plaza gratis en el instituto.

Complete the sentences below. Write the correct letter in each box.

28 Rosalía says she …

A	likes the book as much as ever.
B	preferred the book when she was younger.
C	appreciates the book more now.

☐ **(1 mark)**

29 Rosalía warns people that the novel …

A	contains upsetting themes.
B	will make you laugh out loud.
C	is extremely long.

☐ **(1 mark)**

30 She describes it as …

A	a fun summer read.
B	worth the effort.
C	a book you will not forget.

☐ **(1 mark)**

Answer the following questions in **English**.

31 Who are the typical students at the school? .... **(1 mark)**

32 What is the character Alba's secret? .... **(1 mark)**

Had a go ☐ **Nearly there** ☐ **Nailed it!** ☐   Practice papers

Interview feedback

Read the comments that Mario received from the boss, Sara Martínez, after his interview.

> Estimado Mario
>
> Gracias por asistir a la entrevista el lunes pasado. Tengo que informarte que, aunque eras un candidato muy fuerte, no hemos podido darte el trabajo, lo siento.
>
> Aquí te ofrezco un comentario sobre lo bueno de tu entrevista y mis consejos sobre las cosas que puedes hacer para mejorar en el futuro.
>
> Llegaste con tiempo y vestido adecuadamente para una entrevista formal. Te presentaste como simpático y abierto, y tuve la impresión de que te llevarías bien con los otros compañeros en el equipo.
>
> Cuando te hice preguntas, no parecías saber mucho de la empresa ni del trabajo que hacemos. Es muy importante buscar información sobre la compañía antes de la entrevista. Una pregunta típica es siempre "¿Por qué quieres el trabajo?", y si no entiendes la función de la empresa, no podrás contestar.
>
> Tus dos primeras preguntas trataron de las vacaciones y el salario. Esto no da una buena impresión. Los empresarios necesitan creer que lo que te interesa más es el empleo.

Answer the following questions in **English**.

33 What news does Mario find out at the start of the letter?

.... **(1 mark)**

34 What advice does Sara say she will give him?

.... **(1 mark)**

35 How did Sara feel Mario would fit in at work?

.... **(1 mark)**

36 What was **one** impression that Mario gave when Sara asked him questions?

.... **(1 mark)**

SECTION B

Translation into English

Translate these sentences into **English**.

Mi hermano es muy listo y se parece mucho a mi padre.

....

Los mexicanos están orgullosos de sus fiestas como el Día de los Muertos.

....

Acabo de dar un paseo al lado del río.

....

La plaza de toros ya no se usa para corridas.

....

Prefiero ver los partidos en vivo en el estadio.

....

(10 marks)
TOTAL FOR PAPER = 50 MARKS

Practice papers

Had a go ☐ Nearly there ☐ Nailed it! ☐

Paper 4: Writing (Higher)

In the real exam, you will write your answers on the question paper. Here, you will need to write some answers on your own paper.

SECTION A

Translation into Spanish

1 Translate the following sentences into **Spanish**.

   We usually get on very well with our grandparents.

   ....

   Sometimes I get up late at the weekends.

   ....

   I am going to read all the options before choosing my subjects.

   ....

   She did not want to go out yesterday because it was cold.

   ....

   The good thing about my region is the climate.

   ....

   (10 marks)

SECTION B

An article

2 Choose either Question 2(a) or Question 2(b).

(a) Write an article about home and the environment. You **must** include the following points: • what you and your friends do in your area • something you did recently to help the local environment • what your ideal home would be like.	(b) Write an article about education. You **must** include the following points: • what you think about your school • a trip that you went on with school • what you will study in the future.

Write your answer in **Spanish**. You should aim to write approximately **90** words. **(15 marks)**

SECTION C

A post / An article

3 Choose either Question 3(a) or Question 3(b).

(a) Write a post for a Spanish website about festivals and celebrations. You **must** include the following points: • the positive aspects of festivals • something you did in the past to make a birthday special.	(b) Write an article about technology. You **must** include the following points: • the negative aspects of social media • an event when technology solved a big problem.

Write your answer in **Spanish**. You should aim to write approximately **150** words. **(25 marks)**

Answers

The answers to the Speaking and Writing activities below are sample answers – there are many ways you could answer these questions.

1. Introducing yourself
1 B, D, E
2 (a) It is in the month of July.
   (b) She lives in the north of the country.
   (c) On 25th December

2. Physical descriptions
1 (a) B (b) A (c) C (d) A
2 (a) tall, glasses (b) eyes, feet (c) hair, fat (d) slim / thin, hands

3. Character descriptions
1 (a) C (b) D (c) B (d) A (e) D (f) B
2 Me gustaría ser trabajador/a y responsable.
   No soy muy deportivo/a, pero soy alegre.
   Creo que soy simpático/a y divertido/a, con una actitud positiva y optimista.
   Mis amigos dicen que soy listo/a.
   Fui a la casa de mi amigo/a la semana pasada y lo pasamos bien.

4. Family
1 B, C, F
2 Sample answer:
En la primera foto hay once personas; creo que todos son miembros de la misma familia. Están los abuelos, los padres y los hijos. Están en la cocina de una casa y en la mesa hay comida y fruta y vasos. En mi opinión es una celebración, como un cumpleaños, por ejemplo. Todos están muy contentos y alegres.
En la segunda foto, dos niños están con sus padres en el salón. Tienen un pequeño perro. Uno de los padres está leyendo una historia y tiene un libro en la mano.

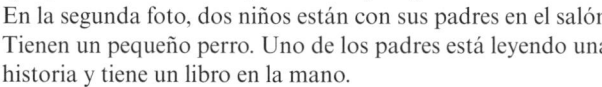

Sample answers to follow-on questions:
(a) Mi familia no es muy numerosa, somos cuatro en total. Vivo con mi padre, mi madrastra y mi hermana mayor.
(b) Me parezco bastante a mi hermana porque las dos somos altas y tenemos el pelo rubio.
(c) Me gustaría mucho tener mi propio piso un día y ser independiente.
(d) No sé, posiblemente, pero no estoy segura.

5. What makes a good friend
1 Read aloud text & sample answers to follow-on questions:
(a) Un amigo perfecto te ayuda si tienes problemas y te hace reír cuando estás triste. También te escucha cuando necesitas hablar.
(b) Me gusta ver películas, ir de compras y escuchar música con mis amigos.
(c) Mi mejor amiga es alegre y divertida.
(d) Mando mensajes en mi móvil.
2 My best friend helps me a lot.
   I like to think that I am a good friend.
   A perfect friend always accepts you as you are.
   Friendship is very important for young people.
   There are moments times when your friend needs to tell you the truth.

6. Relationships
1 (a) B (b) C (c) A (d) C (e) A (f) B

2 Sample answer:
Mi mejor amigo tiene el pelo corto y los ojos grises. Es activo y divertido, y me hace reír mucho. Voy de compras con mis amigos al centro comercial y jugamos al fútbol en el parque. Uno de mis amigos, David, es perezoso y eso me molesta. Creo que soy un buen amigo.

7. Helping a friend
1 1 Mi mejor amigo me ayuda.
   2 Mis compañeros de clase me evitaron.
   3 Su conducta hacia nosotros cambió mucho.
   4 La amistad es esencial cuando eres joven.
   5 Tienes que dejar de fumar ahora.
2 Sample answer:
Hay dos personas en la primera foto, un chico con el pelo corto y marrón y una chica con el pelo largo y marrón. El chico lleva una camisa azul y blanca y la chica lleva una camiseta azul. Creo que son estudiantes.
En la segunda foto, hay dos chicas. Las dos tienen el pelo largo y marrón. Una de las chicas lleva una camisa azul. Está muy triste.

Sample answers to follow-on questions:
(a) Escucho sus problemas. Siempre guardo sus secretos y a veces ayudo con sus deberes.
(b) Me llevo muy bien con mis amigos. Tenemos los mismos intereses y lo pasamos bien juntos.
(c) Casi nunca discutimos, pero discutí con un amigo cuando le presté un libro y lo perdió.
(d) Son muy simpáticos en general, pero algunos son aburridos.

8. Food and drink
1 (a) B (b) C (c) B (d) C
2 Sample answer:
Mi comida favorita es el pescado con patatas fritas, pero también me gustan las hamburguesas con ensalada. No me gustan mucho las cosas dulces.
El sábado pasado preparé una paella en casa para mi familia. ¡Pasé horas en la cocina! Me gustó bastante, pero mi hermano pensó que estaba un poco fría.
Para el cumpleaños de mi madre, la semana próxima, quiero preparar algo especial. Voy a hacer un plato de pollo con verduras porque es su favorito. No le gusta comer en restaurantes, prefiere cenar en casa.

9. Healthy eating
1 Sample answer:
En la primera foto hay una familia a la mesa en la cocina. Están los padres y sus dos hijos. Están tomando una comida muy sana. En la mesa hay mucha fruta y un montón de ensalada. La familia está muy contenta y todos están sonriendo. En la segunda foto, veo a dos amigas que comen juntas en la cocina. Están tomando una comida muy poco sana. Comen hamburguesas y patatas fritas y están bebiendo cola. Una chica lleva una camisa roja y la otra lleva una camiseta amarilla.

Sample answers to follow-on questions:
T: ¿Qué comida te gusta preparar?
S: Me gusta preparar ensaladas porque es muy fácil y rápido.
T: ¿Qué vas a comer este fin de semana?
S: Voy a comer comida mexicana. ¡Me encanta!
T: ¿Qué comiste para tu último cumpleaños?
S: Comí pollo con patatas fritas en un restaurante con mis amigos.

T: ¿Quién prepara las comidas en tu casa?
S: Mi padrastro prepara las comidas en general, pero yo ayudo a veces.
T: ¿Qué comida no te gusta?
S: Odio los huevos.

2 Read aloud text & sample answers to follow-on questions:
(a) Una dieta sana tiene una variedad de comida. Por ejemplo, se puede comer carne, pescado y fruta. Se puede beber agua y leche.
(b) La comida basura es mala para la salud. Odio las hamburguesas y las patatas fritas. No me gustan los caramelos.
(c) No me gusta la comida en mi instituto. No es sana.
(d) Me gusta mucho la comida china.

10. Sport and exercise
1 (a) C2 (b) E1 (c) A3
2 Sample answer:
T: ¿Qué ejercicio te gusta hacer?
S: Mi deporte favorito es el fútbol.
T: ¿Y cuándo juegas?
S: Juego todos los sábados.
T: Ah sí. ¿Con quiénes?
S: Juego con mis amigos.
T: Vale. ¿Dónde jugáis?
S: Normalmente en el parque.
T: Muy bien.
S: ¿Te gusta el deporte?
T: Mucho, especialmente nadar.

11. Physical wellbeing
1 Sample answer:
En la primera foto hay un hombre joven en la cama. Son las dos menos veinte de la mañana, pero no duerme. Está mirando su móvil y podría estar chateando con alguien o buscando información en Internet. No es una buena idea usar la tecnología antes de dormirte. Creo que el chico va a estar muy cansado por la mañana.
En la segunda foto, dos personas están corriendo por el bosque. Hay una mujer y un hombre y llevan ropa deportiva. Están muy en forma porque les gusta correr y hacer ejercicio. Hay un camino en el bosque y muchos árboles.
Sample answers to follow-on questions:
(a) Creo que como una dieta equilibrada, bebo suficiente agua y duermo bien.
(b) El fin de semana pasado, fui a pasear en el bosque con mi perro.
(c) Voy a ir al gimnasio y también iré a la piscina.
(d) Durante la semana me acuesto a las diez, pero me voy a la cama más tarde los fines de semana.
2 Mi hermano duerme muy bien cada noche / todas las noches.
Me gusta pasar tiempo al aire libre.
Bebí mucha agua ayer.
El sol puede hacer daño a tu piel / a la piel.
Está muy cansada hoy.

12. Mental wellbeing
1 (a) A (b) A (c) C (d) B (e) C (f) B
2 I like painting because it's very easy.
My grandfather always listens to me.
When I feel sad / upset, I talk to my friends.
I helped my brother when he had a problem.
Family is very important in my life.

13. Role models in sport
1 (a) She was the first female referee in a World Cup match in men's football.
(b) The line judges / assistant referees were also women.
(c) Girls were not allowed to play football.
(d) She thinks that although there is more equality nowadays, there is still some way to go.
(e) B
2 Juego para el equipo de fútbol de mi instituto.
Me encanta el deporte porque me ayuda a mantenerme en forma.
Disfruto de la amistad con los miembros del equipo.
La semana pasada ganamos un partido contra un instituto de otra ciudad / otro pueblo.
Este sábado creo que perderemos / vamos a perder contra un equipo muy bueno.

14. Sporting events
1 (a) C (b) A (c) B
2 Sample answer:
En la primera foto hay cuatro personas, dos chicos y dos chicas. Están en casa y están viendo un partido de fútbol en la televisión. Creo que el partido es muy emocionante y su equipo está ganando.
En la segunda foto, hay un partido de baloncesto en un estadio. Uno de los equipos lleva ropa amarilla y el otro equipo juega en ropa blanca.
Sample answer to follow-on questions:
(a) Creo que el fútbol es el deporte más emocionante.
(b) Hay muchos gimnasios y un gran estadio de fútbol. También hay piscinas.
(c) A veces. En verano me gusta ver el tenis en la tele.
(d) Es muy emocionante cuando estás en el estadio porque hay mucha gente y mucho ruido.

15. School subjects
1 (a) A (b) C (c) B
2 Read aloud text and sample answers to follow-on questions:
(a) Estudio inglés, matemáticas, ciencias, español, historia y dibujo.
(b) Me parece muy difícil. No saco buenas notas y creo que no voy a aprobar el examen en verano.
(c) Me gustan todas mis asignaturas, pero creo que el dibujo me gusta menos. La profesora me da muchos deberes cada semana.
(d) Espero continuar con el inglés, el español y la historia. Pero depende de los exámenes.

16. School subjects – likes and dislikes
1 1 Normalmente saca buenas notas en biología.
2 No tengo talento en dibujo pero es divertido.
3 La tecnología es aburrida a veces.
4 La historia es una asignatura muy útil.
5 Mi clase favorita es educación física.
2 Sample answer:
Tengo mucha suerte porque me gustan todas mis asignaturas.
Me encanta el español porque las clases son divertidas y me gusta practicar el idioma cuando voy de vacaciones a España.
Dejé el dibujo en el tercer curso porque es difícil para mí y no sacaba buenas notas en las pruebas. No me interesan nada las actividades artísticas.
El año próximo voy a continuar con el español, el inglés y una asignatura más. No sé cuál voy a escoger. Voy a ver mis notas después de los exámenes y luego decidiré.

17. The school day
1 (a) B (b) A (c) C (d) C (e) A (f) B
2 Sample answer:
En mi instituto, la primera clase empieza a las ocho y media y terminamos a las tres y veinticinco.
El martes pasado decidí ir al instituto a pie porque hacía sol. Normalmente voy en coche con mi padre pero el martes fui a pie con mi amigo. El viernes mi padre trabajó en casa y yo fui al instituto en bicicleta.
Mañana voy a ir en coche porque tengo que llevar mi equipo de deporte. Hay educación física primero, y luego matemáticas, historia y ciencias. Por la tarde, tenemos dibujo. (90 words)

18. School facilities
1 (a) P (b) P+N (c) P
2 Sample answer:
  1 Hay cuatro jóvenes.
  2 Están en la biblioteca del instituto.
  3 Hay una mesa.
  4 Los chicos están estudiando.
  5 También están buscando información en Internet.

19. School uniform
1 Sample answer:
En la primera foto hay un grupo de nueve estudiantes con su profesora en una clase de música. Los estudiantes llevan uniforme: una chaqueta azul y una camisa azul. Los chicos también llevan corbatas. En la segunda foto hay cuatro alumnos en la calle cerca de un gran autobús. Los chicos van al instituto y están hablando.

Sample answers to follow-on questions:
(a) Tenemos una chaqueta roja oscura y una falda o pantalones grises. Los zapatos tienen que ser negros. No llevamos jersey, pero la corbata es blanca y negra.
(b) Llevamos pantalones cortos negros y camisetas blancas.
(c) Me gustaría cambiar la camisa, que es azul. Prefiero llevar una camisa blanca con los colores del resto del uniforme.
(d) No, no es cómodo y creo que es feo. Me gustaría llevar mi ropa normal.
2 (a) C (b) B (c) A

20. Activities in class
1 Read aloud text & sample answers to follow-on questions:
(a) Me gusta tener una variedad de actividades. A veces me gusta el trabajo en equipo pero otras veces prefiero hacer el trabajo solo.
(b) Me gusta buscar información en Internet y hacer ejercicios en línea. Algunos de los juegos educativos son bastante divertidos.
(c) Leo los libros de texto y hago ejercicios en línea.
(d) Salgo al patio a comer un bocadillo.

2 Sample answer:
En mi instituto tenemos cuatro clases por la mañana y dos por la tarde. Hay un recreo después de la segunda clase.
Me gustan más las clases de español porque hacemos una gran variedad de actividades y nunca es aburrido.
Por ejemplo, la semana pasada, hablamos de las vacaciones y aprendimos nuevas palabras. También hicimos ejercicios de escuchar y leer usando los ordenadores.
La semana próxima, en la clase de religión vamos a tener una discusión. Antes de la clase tenemos que buscar información y preparar nuestras ideas y opiniones. (90 words)

21. School rules
1 1 Las normas son justas.
  2 No podemos comer chicle.
  3 Tenemos que llevar el uniforme correcto.
  4 Está prohibido correr en el colegio.

2 Tienes que / Debes / Hay que hacer los deberes todos los días / cada día.
No debes / No hay que / No se debe tirar basura en el patio.
No puedes traer / llevar el móvil a la clase.
Siempre debemos tener el equipo necesario.
Mi amigo / a llegó tarde al instituto ayer.

22. The good and the bad about school
1 (a) the library (b) (lots of) new computers
  (c) timetable (d) start too early
2 El director es muy justo. / La directora es muy justa.
Aprobé el examen la semana pasada.
Podemos pedir ayuda en clase.
Algo que me gusta mucho es el uso de la tecnología.
Algunos / unos profesores nos dan demasiados deberes. **OR**
Algunas / unas profesoras nos dan demasiados deberes.

23. School clubs and activities
1 (a) C (b) B (c) C (d) A (e) B (f) A
2 (a) When she was living with an English family. / When she spent two weeks with an English family
  (b) After school / After classes
  (c) **Two of**: Dance classes, English lessons, learning to play an instrument
  (d) You have to pay; schools that organise them are private.

24. How to be a good student
1 A, C, F
2 Sample answer:
En la primera foto hay una clase de unos quince estudiantes, chicos y chicas, y su profesor. Algunos tienen portátiles o tabletas y otros solo tienen bolígrafos y papel. No llevan uniforme. La clase parece muy interesante y divertida.

En la otra foto, dos chicas están estudiando juntas en casa. Una de las chicas tiene el pelo marrón y la otra es rubia. Tienen el pelo largo. Están leyendo información y hablando de los deberes que tienen que hacer.
Sample answers to follow-on questions:
(a) Llevo el material correcto a la clase, siempre escucho al profesor y nunca hablo cuando el profesor está hablando. Hago mis deberes con tiempo y nunca los entrego sin terminar.
(b) Leí y escribí mucho, practiqué con ejemplos del examen del pasado y mi madre me ayudó, haciéndome preguntas que tuve que contestar sin mirar el libro de texto.
(c) Creo que normalmente no es una buena idea. A veces solo una de las personas está haciendo el trabajo y la otra no aprende mucho.
(d) Uso información de Internet todo el tiempo. Hay muchos sitios educativos muy buenos y hay actividades y ejercicios para ayudarte a aprender y repasar.

25. Options at 16
1 (a) C (b) A (c) C (d) B
2 Read aloud text & sample answers to follow-on questions:
(a) Mis asignaturas favoritas son el inglés, la historia y el dibujo. Son interesantes y bastante fáciles. Saco buenas notas en estas asignaturas.

(b) No me gustan nada. Son muy difíciles y estoy muy nerviosa cuando tengo exámenes.
(c) Puedo continuar con mis estudios aquí en el instituto o estudiar algo diferente.
(d) Quiero estudiar ciencias.

26. Future study plans
1. (a) the vocational / professional training courses
   (b) it / the college is far from home
   (c) the technology resources
   (d) the sports facilities
2. Sample answer:
   T: ¿Qué planes tienes para tus estudios el año próximo?
   S: Tengo la intención de ir a un instituto local para estudiar matemáticas, ciencias y español.
   T: ¿Cuáles son tus razones para escoger este curso?
   S: Me gustan las ciencias en el instituto y es mejor estudiar matemáticas también porque las dos asignaturas van bien juntas. Quiero estudiar español simplemente porque me gusta, y será una clase muy diferente de las otras.
   T: ¿Quieres ir a la universidad?
   S: Sí, tengo muchas ganas de ir a la universidad porque he decidido que quiero ser médica en el futuro. Entonces, necesito estudiar medicina y sacar un título.
   T: ¿Cuáles son los beneficios de ir a la universidad?
   S: Creo que puedes conseguir un trabajo mejor pagado si tienes un título de la universidad y tienes más opciones de trabajo en general. También, hay muchas actividades sociales y oportunidades interesantes.
   T: ¿Cuáles son los aspectos negativos?
   S: Son más años de estudio sin ganar un salario, y esto puede ser duro. Sé que muchos estudiantes trabajan al mismo tiempo que estudian, pero esto crea mucha presión.
   T: ¿Qué otras cosas te gustaría aprender en el futuro?
   S: Hay muchas cosas que me gustaría aprender. Quiero aprender a hacer mi propia ropa y quiero aprender otro idioma, como el francés. El año próximo, voy a aprender a conducir.

27. Future plans
1.
   1. Voy a abrir una cuenta bancaria.
   2. Me gustaría vivir en otra comunidad.
   3. Mi sueño es viajar por el mundo.
   4. Quiero hacer una carrera universitaria.
   5. Mi objetivo es tener mucho éxito.
2. Sample answer:
En este momento estudio ocho asignaturas diferentes y mis favoritas son la educación física, el inglés y la historia. Mis estudios van bien y saco buenas notas en las pruebas, aunque no en matemáticas porque no las comprendo. Soy una persona muy activa y me gustan muchos deportes diferentes. Pero también me interesa aprender sobre el cuerpo y cómo funciona. Por eso disfruto mucho las clases de educación física.
Espero ir a la universidad cuando tenga dieciocho años. Lo bueno de ir a la universidad es estudiar tu asignatura preferida durante tres o cuatro años y salir al final con un título. Lo difícil será pasar más años sin salario. El septiembre próximo continuaré con mis tres asignaturas favoritas y creo que iré a la universidad para estudiar deporte. Pienso que me gustaría ser profesor de educación física en una escuela. Creo que es un trabajo muy importante.

28. Part-time jobs and money
1. (a) Sunday(s)
   (b) At the checkout / on the tills (1) in a supermarket (1)
   (c) Speak to the boss
   (d) 9 o'clock
2. Sample answer:
   1. Hay una chica joven.
   2. Trabaja en un café.
   3. El hombre está comprando un café y un bocadillo.
   4. El hombre lleva una camisa azul.
   5. Está pagando con tarjeta.

29. Opinions about jobs
1. (a) M (b) M (c) A (d) P (e) P (f) A
2. Read aloud text & sample answers to follow-on questions:
   (a) Trabajar con otras personas y tener compañeros simpáticos. También es importante llevarte bien con el jefe o la jefa.
   (b) Me interesa ser policía porque pagan bien.
   (c) No quiero trabajar al aire libre porque el tiempo es muy malo y no me gustaría hacer trabajo físico.
   (d) Creo que trabajar en un país como España es una buena idea.

30. The pros and cons of different jobs
1. Sample answer:
En la primera foto podemos ver una oficina moderna con una gran ventana y una escalera que va a la puerta principal. Hay seis personas en la foto y creo que son las nueve de la mañana porque tres de las personas acaban de llegar al trabajo. Un hombre ha venido en bicicleta y va a guardar la bici en la oficina para mantenerla segura. En la segunda foto hay una mujer trabajando. Está en un laboratorio. Es científica. Es muy inteligente y su trabajo es muy importante y útil.
Sample answers to follow-on questions:
(a) No me importa trabajar en una oficina, pero el trabajo tiene que ser interesante. Si estoy haciendo algo que me gusta, entonces el lugar no es importante. Otro aspecto clave es tener compañeros simpáticos.
(b) El fin de semana pasado lavé el coche de mis padres y me dieron dinero. También cuidé a los niños de la vecina el viernes por la noche.
(c) No quiero ser profesor. Sería bueno tener vacaciones largas, pero tienes que trabajar muchas horas y es un puesto de mucha responsabilidad.
(d) Quería ser actor y salir en la tele o en películas. Me gustaba mucho actuar en obras de teatro en el instituto.

2. I want to work in an office with modern equipment.
There are lots of rules in this company / firm.
My sister hopes to be a scientist or a teacher.
I went abroad six times when I worked for the company.
I would not like to be a doctor; it's too difficult.

31. Job adverts
1. Necesito llamar a la empresa / compañía.
Soy trabajador/a y tengo una actitud positiva.
Busco / Estoy buscando información online.
Mi hermana encontró un trabajo en el periódico.
La empresa / compañía quiere gente con experiencia.
2. Sample answer:
   T: ¿Qué tipo de trabajo quieres?
   S: Me gustaría ser periodista y escribir artículos.
   T: ¿Y tu personalidad es apropiada para eso?
   S: Tengo buenos conocimientos informáticos y me gusta escribir.
   T: ¿Te gustaría trabajar en el extranjero?
   S: Me encantaría trabajar en el extranjero porque podría usar mis idiomas.
   T: ¿Dónde vas a buscar más información?
   S: Voy a buscar más información online.
   T: Buena idea.
   S: ¿Te gusta tu trabajo?
   T: Sí, claro.

32. Applying for jobs
1 (a) B (b) C (c) C
2 1 Voy a llamar a este número.
   2 El jefe es estricto.
   3 Tus compañeros parecen muy capaces.
   4 La empresa está lejos /de aquí.

33. Preparing for interviews
1 Sample answer:
En la primera foto hay cinco personas sentadas en una línea. Creo que están esperando una entrevista. Todos están muy serios y probablemente están nerviosos. Uno de los hombres está mirando su reloj.

Listen to the recording

En la otra foto una chica tiene una entrevista. Está en una oficina y creo que está nerviosa. Hay cuatro jefes y parecen muy serios. La chica lleva un traje gris y tiene el pelo marrón. En la oficina, todo es blanco, las paredes, las sillas, la mesa y el reloj. No me gustaría trabajar allí.
Sample answers to follow-on questions:
(a) Me gustaría trabajar en un hotel o restaurante en Barcelona. Podría practicar el español hablando con los clientes y ganar dinero al mismo tiempo. Durante mis días libres, iría a la playa.
(b) Fui a una entrevista de trabajo y llevé un traje negro y una camisa blanca.
(c) Tienes que buscar información sobre el trabajo y la empresa. También hay que pensar en cómo vas a contestar las preguntas típicas.
(d) Tienes que llegar con tiempo y es mejor ser natural. Es una buena idea hacer preguntas al final.
2 Yesterday I went to the Tourist Office for an interview.
I wore a grey suit, a white shirt and black shoes.
I felt quite nervous, but the boss was nice / friendly.
There were lots of questions, but I could answer with confidence / confidently.
He / She told me that they would call me this Thursday to tell me if I have been successful.

34. Working to help others
1 (a) Reads (stories) to children
  (b) Does the gardening / Works in the garden
  (c) Organises games **or** Organises exercises (Or both)
2 Sample answers:
  1 Hay un profesor.
  2 Está en una clase.
  3 Está ayudando a los niños.
  4 Lleva una camiseta azul.
  5 Los niños tienen cinco años.

35. Free-time activities
1 1 A veces voy al cine.
   2 Ver la televisión es aburrido.
   3 Siempre me fascinan las obras extranjeras.
   4 Me interesa el ciclismo.
2 Read aloud text & sample answers to follow-on questions:
(a) Me gusta mucho hacer deportes y actividades activas. El deporte que me gusta más es el fútbol. También me gusta correr y, de vez en cuando, juego al tenis con mi hermana.

Listen to the recording

(b) Juego al fútbol los miércoles por la tarde en las clases de educación física, y también con el equipo los sábados. Me voy a correr los domingos por la mañana. Solo jugamos al tenis en verano cuando hace buen tiempo.
(c) Hay un centro de deportes que tiene una gran piscina. Hay un parque donde se puede jugar al fútbol. No tenemos un cine, pero hay uno bastante cerca.
(d) Me gusta leer y escuchar música. A veces juego a los videojuegos, pero no mucho.

36. Music and dance
1 (a) B (b) C (c) A (d) A (e) B (f) B
2 Sample answer:
La música que me gusta más es la música pop porque es alegre. Odio la música rap, es horrible.
Escucho música cuando estoy en mi dormitorio y también cuando estoy haciendo mis deberes.
No toco ningún instrumento. Quiero ver un concierto de Taylor Swift porque me gusta mucho su voz.

37. Music and dance events
1 (a) B (b) A (c) C (d) B
2 I have (got) the tickets for the concert.
I think it is going to be very exciting.
My favourite group will play their latest songs.
Yesterday I listened to their music and read the words / lyrics.
We are going to have a very / really good time, I am sure.

38. Reading
1 Sample answer:
La primera foto es de un chico con el pelo marrón y rizado*. Lleva una camiseta blanca y una camisa azul. Tiene unos dieciocho años, creo. Está en la cocina de su casa, sentado a la mesa, y está leyendo una novela. Hay un vaso de agua.

Listen to the recording

El chico tiene la boca abierta y creo que está muy sorprendido.
La segunda foto es de una profesora que lee una historia a un pequeño grupo de niños. Los niños escuchan y están sonriendo. Están muy interesados en la historia y parecen muy contentos.
*If you know vocabulary that is not on the AQA list, you can use it – for example here *rizado* ('curly') is used successfully.
Sample answers to follow-on questions:
(a) Me gusta bastante. Cuando era joven, leía todo el tiempo, pero ahora es difícil encontrar tiempo. Y, claro, siempre hay muchas otras cosas que se pueden hacer.
(b) Leí una novela sobre una chica que viaja en el tiempo y termina viviendo en el pasado. Me gustó mucho porque fue emocionante y el personaje principal me hizo reír.
(c) Creo que aprendes mucho y también desarrollas tu imaginación.
(d) Hay muchas otras actividades que podemos hacer, en casa, al aire libre o en la ciudad. También, muchos jóvenes prefieren actividades más sociales que pueden hacer con sus amigos.
2 No me gusta leer (los) periódicos.
Este libro tiene demasiadas páginas.
El personaje principal es muy simpático.
Mi hermano prefiere las novelas de ciencia ficción.
La semana pasada leí una historia con un final muy triste.

39. Television
1 Sample answer:
Me gusta ver las series de humor o las películas de acción. Nunca veo los programas de cocina, no me interesan nada, y no veo las noticias mucho porque son tristes. Me encanta el deporte y más que nada me gusta ver los partidos de fútbol porque siempre son divertidos y emocionantes.
La semana pasada vi un programa sobre animales y la naturaleza. Fue muy educativo.
Este fin de semana voy a ver un programa sobre la historia de España. Será útil para mis estudios.
2 (a) B (b) C

40. The cinema
1. Read aloud text & sample answers to follow-on questions:
   (a) Mi película favorita es *El señor de los anillos*. Me encanta el libro y creo que la película es estupenda también.
   (b) Normalmente prefiero ver las películas en casa, en Netflix y otros sitios. A veces, cuando hay una película que es mejor en una pantalla grande, entonces vale la pena ir al cine.
   (c) Odio las películas de miedo. No puedo dormir después.
   (d) Siempre voy con una amiga o un grupo de amigos.
2. Mi película favorita tiene unas canciones maravillosas. Es la historia de una mujer que quiere ser una estrella famosa. También ganó muchos premios.
   A veces es divertida, pero tiene unos momentos tristes al final. Voy a verla otra vez este fin de semana.

41. What's the story?
1. (a) comedy / funny (b) action (c) girlfriend
2. Sample answer:
En la primera foto hay un hombre sentado en el salón de su casa. Es un salón bonito y moderno con paredes azules. El hombre está muy cómodo y está relajándose. Lleva una camisa y pantalones azules y zapatillas de deporte. Tiene el pelo negro. Está viendo un programa en la tele, que tiene una pantalla muy grande. El programa podría ser un documental.
En la segunda foto, hay muchas personas en el cine. Están viendo una película muy graciosa y se están riendo mucho.
Sample answers to follow-on questions:
(a) Me encanta ir al cine porque la pantalla es muy grande y hay un ambiente especial. También el sonido es mejor.
(b) Fui con mis amigos el sábado pasado. Lo pasamos muy bien. Cuando era pequeño, iba con mis padres y mi hermana para ver las películas familiares.
(c) Me encanta la serie *Cosas extrañas* (en inglés 'Stranger Things'). Es una serie americana pero es popular en muchos países. Se trata de un grupo de niños que descubren otro mundo.
(d) Voy a ver el fútbol en vivo en la tele el martes, porque mi equipo juega y es un partido importante.

42. Everyday life
1. (a) B (b) C (c) A
2. Tomo mi desayuno en la cocina.
Normalmente me levanto a las ocho.
Sale de (la) casa y coge el autobús.
Hago mis deberes después de la cena.
El fin de semana pasado vi la televisión con mi familia.

43. Meals at home
1. (a) at different times (b) grandmother
   (c) she refuses to / won't eat her greens / the vegetables.
   (d) a lighter meal
2. I have a sandwich when I return / go back home.
I take fruit to school to eat during break.
Yesterday we had dinner / the evening meal at ten (o'clock).
I am going to serve chicken with chips.
I like to help prepare / I like helping to prepare food / the meal / dinner / lunch.

44. Celebrations
1. 1 Compramos un pastel de cumpleaños.
   2 Voy a sacar muchas fotos.
   3 Hice un plato de bistec.
   4 Fue una noche muy emocionante.
2. Sample answers:
   1 Es el cumpleaños del padre.
   2 Está abriendo sus regalos.
   3 El padre está con sus tres hijos.
   4 Están en el salón de su casa.
   5 Hay tarjetas sobre la mesa.

45. Customs and festivals
1. (a) flowers and books / the man gives flowers and the woman gives a book
   (b) They are filled with stalls selling books.
   (c) The book sellers arrive to set up their stalls.
   (d) An author comes and signs copies of their book. / a book signing by an author
   (e) It was when the fiesta / festival started.
   (f) to commemorate the deaths of Cervantes and Shakespeare
2. A, B, D

46. Spanish festivals
1. (a) P (b) P+N (c) N (d) P
2. (a) P (b) N (c) P (d) F

47. Latin American festivals
1. (a) **Either** She ceases to be a child. **or** She becomes a woman.
   (b) a long dress
   (c) The girl / She dances the first dance with her father.
   (d) It is the last doll of childhood. / It means she is no longer a child.
   (e) She changes her shoes for high heels.
2. Sample answer
En la primera foto hay una fiesta alegre y divertida, y hay hombres y mujeres que bailan en la calle. Las mujeres llevan vestidos largos de muchos colores y tienen flores en el pelo. Los hombres llevan camisas y pantalones de colores vivos. La segunda foto es un desfile más serio. En la calle, varias personas ven pasar el desfile que consiste en numerosos hombres en caballos blancos. Los hombres llevan uniformes de color negro y rojo. Al fondo, hay muchos árboles verdes y un edificio alto – creo que son pisos.
Sample answers to follow-on questions:
(a) Me gusta mucho la Tomatina. Creo que es muy divertida y un poco loca. Me gustaría participar un día.
(b) No sé cuánto cuestan, pero deben ser muy caras. Creo que los ayuntamientos tienen que considerar si deberían gastar el dinero en otras cosas más importantes.
(c) Hay mucho ruido y los turistas dejan mucha basura. Durante varios días el pueblo o la ciudad está lleno de personas, y esto puede molestar a los habitantes.
(d) Creo que la gente lo pasa bien cuando hay una fiesta. Sale a la calle y se divierte. También los turistas vienen y gastan mucho dinero en el pueblo.

48. My favourite celebrity
1. (a) A+B (b) A (c) B (d) A+B
2. Sample answer:
Mi grupo favorito se llama *Carolina Durante* y toca música rock y pop. Su nombre es el nombre de una chica que conocieron de jóvenes – es una mujer real y ahora es periodista. El grupo actuó en varios festivales de música y dio conciertos en el extranjero además de en España. En 2019 ganó premios por Mejor canción y Mejor artista nuevo. Voy a escuchar su música esta noche en las redes sociales, pero espero ir a un concierto del grupo este año. Creo que van a tocar en mi ciudad en noviembre.

49. Profile of a celebrity
1. Sample answer:
   T: ¿Quién es tu persona famosa favorita?
   S: Me gusta mucho Harry Styles.
   T: ¿Qué hace?
   S: Es un cantante muy famoso.
   T: ¿Cómo es físicamente?
   S: Tiene el pelo marrón y los ojos verdes.
   T: ¿Dónde ves a esta persona?
   S: Lo veo en YouTube.
   T: Ah claro.
   S: ¿Es buena la televisión en España?
   T: La verás durante tu visita.
2. Sample answer:
   Mi programa favorito es *The Traitors*.
   Es un programa de telerrealidad.
   Hay una serie cada año. Hay tres programas cada semana. Dura tres o cuatro semanas.
   La mujer que presenta el programa se llama Claudia.
   Es muy guapa y muy divertida. Tiene el pelo negro. Me gusta mucho la ropa que lleva.

50. Celebrities as role models
1. (a) A (b) E (c) H (d) A (e) E (f) H
2. Publicaron una foto de la novia del cantante en una revista.
   El comportamiento del jugador ha tenido un impacto en la imagen del club.
   Respeto al músico porque es un buen modelo (a seguir).
   Va a usar su dinero para ayudar a otras personas.
   La banda / El grupo da un buen ejemplo a los jóvenes.

51. TV reality shows
1. Read aloud text & sample answers to follow-on questions
   (a) Me gustan algunos, pero otros son aburridos y tontos. Me gustan los concursos de canciones.
   (b) Normalmente son animadas, pero me molestan.
   (c) Me gusta la idea porque me gustaría tener mucho dinero. Sin embargo, hay mucha presión.
   (d) Me gustaría. Puede ser emocionante y muy divertido.
2. (a) B (b) E (c) C

52. The good and the bad of being famous
1. Sample answer:
   En la primera foto los periodistas quieren una entrevista con un hombre famoso. El famoso lleva una camisa blanca y gafas de sol. Creo que está contento de contestar sus preguntas. A su lado hay un hombre fuerte que lo protege si hay peligro. En la segunda foto hay cuatro personas. Están de vacaciones en un barco en el mar. Beben vino y parecen felices. Creo que una de las personas es famosa y tiene mucho dinero.
   Sample answers to follow-on questions:
   T: ¿Te gustaría ser muy rico?
   S: Sí, claro. Creo que sería estupendo.
   T: ¿Qué comprarías?
   S: Compraría una casa nueva para mi familia, con una piscina y un gimnasio. Luego iría de viaje con mis dos mejores amigos.
   T: ¿Qué tipo de música prefieres?
   S: Me gusta la música rock y algo de música pop.
   T: ¿Te gusta ir a conciertos?
   S: Sí, me encanta. Es muy emocionante ver a tus cantantes favoritos en concierto.
   T: ¿Qué haces en tu tiempo libre?
   S: Hago deporte, juego a los videojuegos y veo series en Netflix.
   T: ¿Cómo celebraste tu último cumpleaños?
   S: Fui a un parque temático con mis amigos y por la tarde fui a un restaurante con mi familia.
   T: ¿Qué planes tienes para este fin de semana?
   S: Voy a ir al centro comercial el sábado, y el domingo iré a la piscina.
2. (a) P (b) P+N (c) N (d) P

53. Plans for the holidays
1. (a) D, E (b) F, H (c) B, C
2. (a) Swimming pool
   (b) Too many people (on a Saturday)
   (c) Monday
   (d) The pool is closed (for cleaning)
   (e) A bike ride
   (f) Lunch / sandwiches and a drink

54. Holiday preferences
1. (a) A2 (b) E3 (c) B4
2. Sample answer:
   T: ¿Qué lugar del mundo te gustaría más visitar?
   S: Me gustaría ir a Sudamérica. Creo que sería increíble visitar países como México y Argentina. Sería una experiencia maravillosa que nunca olvidaría.
   T: ¿Te gusta pasar las vacaciones en tu país?
   S: Me encanta pasar una semana en junio en mi país, en el campo o en la costa. Después, iría a España una semana en octubre cuando todavía hace buen tiempo.
   T: ¿Dónde prefieres pasar las vacaciones?
   S: Prefiero la costa. Me encanta estar al lado del mar para tomar el sol en la playa. Normalmente hay muchas actividades que hacer también.
   T: ¿Qué piensas de pasar las vacaciones en una casa en el campo?
   S: Creo que sería muy aburrido. No hay mucho que hacer, y sería demasiado tranquilo.
   T: ¿Con quién prefieres ir de vacaciones?
   S: Siempre voy de vacaciones con mi familia y es muy divertido porque me llevo bien con mis hermanos y hacemos muchas actividades juntos. Pero un día me gustaría ir de vacaciones con mis amigos. Creo que lo pasaría muy bien.
   T: ¿En qué estación del año prefieres ir de vacaciones?
   S: Si voy de vacaciones en mi país, prefiero ir en verano porque hace mejor tiempo. Pero si voy al extranjero, a un país como España, a veces hace demasiado calor en verano y la primavera sería ideal.

55. Types of holidays
1. (a) P (b) L (c) F (d) P (e) F (f) L
2. Sample answer:
   En la primera foto vemos a una familia que está de vacaciones. Hacen camping en un bosque y tienen tiendas de color azul y gris. El padre y el hijo mayor están sentados en sillas y también hay dos niñas. Todos están cerca del fuego. Creo que hace buen tiempo porque llevan camisetas y pantalones cortos.
   En la segunda foto, veo una gran playa llena de personas que toman el sol. Es verano y hace muy buen tiempo. Hace sol y calor y el cielo es azul y sin nubes. Algunas personas están en el mar, pero la mayoría está en la arena.

Sample answers to follow-on questions:
(a) Me encantan. Me gusta mucho estar al lado del mar y tomar el sol en la playa. Nado en el mar y salgo a cenar con la familia por la tarde.
(b) Creo que pueden ser interesantes. Me gusta hacer una variedad de actividades cuando estoy de vacaciones. Es interesante visitar sitios históricos.
(c) No, creo que no. No me gustan los deportes de invierno y odio tener frío. Prefiero ir de vacaciones cuando hace sol y calor.
(d) Me gusta más quedarme en un piso o en una casa porque tienes más espacio y no tienes que comer en el restaurante del hotel. No me gusta nada hacer camping, no es cómodo.

56. Where to stay
1 (a) C (b) A (c) B (d) A (e) B (f) C
2 Las instalaciones en el hotel son excelentes.
Vamos a quedarnos / Nos vamos a quedar en un camping de tres estrellas.
Espero alquilar una casa cerca de la playa.
El piso estaba muy limpio y tenía vistas a la piscina.
Llovió el jueves cuando fuimos al parque temático.

57. Booking accommodation
1 C, D, E
2 1 Quiero una habitación con ducha.
   2 Está enfrente de la playa.
   3 ¿Cuánto es el piso en total?
   4 Los jardines eran pequeños.

58. Holiday activities
1 Sample answer:
  1 En la foto hay ocho personas.
  2 Están en un barco.
  3 Hacen una excursión en el mar.
  4 Algunas personas sacan fotos.
  5 Hace buen tiempo.
2 Read aloud text & sample answers to follow-on questions:
(a) Me gusta tomar el sol en la playa y nadar en la piscina. También me gusta hacer deporte al aire libre.
(b) Me gusta visitar castillos porque son interesantes, pero algunos edificios son un poco aburridos.
(c) Me quedo en casa para ver vídeos.
(d) Me gusta comer la comida típica de la región.

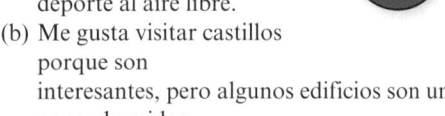

59. Trips and visits
1 Sample answer:
T: Buenos días. ¿Cómo puedo ayudarle?
S: Quiero ir de excursión el viernes, por la mañana.
T: Vale. ¿A qué hora quiere ir?
S: Quiero ir a las diez.
T: Pues hay varias. ¿Qué tipo de excursión busca?
S: Tengo ganas de hacer una excursión en barco porque me gustan las vistas desde el río.
T: Aquí hay una que sería ideal.
S: ¿Cuánto cuestan los billetes?
T: Son ocho euros por persona. ¿Cuál es su opinión del hotel?
S: Me gusta mucho porque es muy cómodo.
T: Vale, gracias.

2 Several days ago, we went on a trip to the mountains (to the) north of the city / town.
We went by bus / coach and the journey took an hour and a half.
We stopped in a village to eat / for lunch and there were flowers everywhere.
Today we are buying / shopping for souvenirs at the market.
I am very keen to visit the castle tomorrow.

60. Giving and asking for directions
1 Sample answer:
T: ¿Qué quieres saber?
S: Por favor ¿a qué hora está abierto el supermercado?
T: A las nueve. ¿Qué quieres comprar?
S: Quiero comprar una camiseta.
T: Muy bien. ¿Qué piensas de la ciudad?
S: Me gusta mucho.
T: ¿Y dónde te quedas?
S: Estamos en el hotel Miramar.
T: Muy bien. ¿Cuándo vuelves a casa?
S: Vuelvo a casa mañana.
T: De acuerdo.

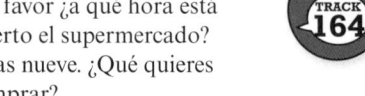

2 (a) Follow the street on the right
  (b) Cross / Go over the bridge
  (c) Take the street to the left
  (d) 50 metres
  (e) A park
  (f) At 7

61. Tourist information
1 1 El puente romano es muy hermoso.
   2 El turismo es esencial aquí.
   3 Van a cerrar la oficina pronto.
   4 Cogimos un horario en la biblioteca.
   5 Tengo ganas de ver el edificio nuevo.
2 Voy a la oficina de turismo.
Queremos una lista de hoteles en la zona / región.
El plano enseña / muestra muchos sitios interesantes.
Pedí información sobre la fiesta.
El castillo no está abierto al público.

62. Tourist attractions
1 We have just spent the day in Barcelona.
Without a doubt it is a beautiful city with lots of places of interest.
I enjoyed walking along the street from the square to the port, with all the stalls of flowers / flower stalls.
It is worth going to see the park and the buildings.
The architecture is very interesting.
2 Sample answer:
Mientras estás aquí sería bueno ir a la ciudad para ver el puerto y los museos en esa zona. Es una zona bonita con muchos edificios interesantes. También tienes que pasar tiempo en el campo porque hay unos caminos hermosos al lado del río y en el valle.
La semana pasada fui a un concierto en el estadio en la ciudad. Había muchos grupos y muchos cantantes allí.
Durante tu visita, ¿por qué no vamos al campo? Podemos ir en bicicleta y llevar la comida para comer al aire libre. ¡Va a ser estupendo!

63. Holiday problems
1 Martina – C   Nicolás – D   Lucía – E
2 Sample answer:
Me gusta hacer viajes diferentes en vacaciones. Es maravilloso estar en la playa cuando hace sol y puedes nadar en el mar. Pero también me encanta hacer turismo y ver todos los sitios de interés en la zona. Cuando vas de vacaciones en este país, siempre hay riesgo de tener mal tiempo porque la lluvia afecta a muchas de las actividades que quieres hacer. Sin embargo, hay mucho que hacer

y numerosas regiones hermosas. Además de esto, me gustan las vacaciones activas, haciendo actividades y deportes diferentes. Un día me gustaría visitar México. Quiero probar la comida y ver las fiestas y costumbres de ese país. La cultura mexicana es muy interesante, y me encantaría estar allí para ver los desfiles del Día de Muertos. También tiene una historia muy rica y se puede ver edificios de hace muchos siglos. Después de ver todo eso, me gustaría terminar en un hotel de lujo con una piscina muy grande.

64. Accommodation problems
1. (a) His wife
   (b) Near the café
   (c) Young people are making noise
   (d) No noise after 10.30 pm
   (e) The receptionist should talk to the young people.
   (f) Move Nicolás to another part of the campsite
2. Hay un problema con la cuenta.
   Las ventanas en el piso están sucias.
   El hotel no tiene (un) restaurante.
   Pedimos una habitación con vistas / vista al mar.
   No estoy contento / a con la cama.

65. Eating out
1. Sample answers:
   T: ¿Qué tipo de comida te gusta?
   S: Me gusta mucho el pescado.
   T: ¿Adónde vas cuando sales a cenar?
   S: Vamos a un restaurante italiano.
   T: ¿Con quién vas?
   S: Normalmente voy con mi familia.
   T: ¡Qué bien!
   S: ¿Tienes un restaurante favorito?
   T: Si, está en mi pueblo. ¿Qué piensas de la comida española?
   S: Me gusta mucho.

   Listen to the recording

2. (a) a table for two
   (b) by the window
   (c) if the rice dish is made with meat / if there is meat in the rice dish
   (d) It is made with vegetables. / It is a vegetarian dish.
   (e) fish and chips
   (f) (a bottle of) water

66. Opinions about food
1. Sample answer:
En la primera foto hay un grupo de amigos, tres mujeres y dos hombres. La chica en el centro lleva gafas. Están en un café. Están tomando hamburguesas y patatas fritas. Están muy contentos. En la segunda foto, hay una chica con el pelo largo y rubio. Lleva una camiseta gris.

Listen to the recording

Sample answers to follow-on questions:
(a) Prefiero la comida sana, como el pescado y las verduras. Como bastante fruta también.
(b) Creo que la comida rápida no es muy sana, pero a veces me gusta tomar una hamburguesa con patatas fritas.
(c) No me gustan mucho las cosas dulces ni los caramelos. Tienen demasiado azúcar.
(d) Tomé una ensalada con pollo, un bocadillo de jamón y una manzana.

2. 1 Yo prefiero / las naranjas españolas.
   2 Ayer hicieron / una paella / muy rica.
   3 Los postres / son demasiado dulces.
   4 Quiero probar / los churros.

67. The weather
1. Sample answers:
   1 Hay dos personas en la foto.
   2 Están en un banco.
   3 Están en un parque.
   4 Hay muchos árboles.
   5 Está lloviendo.
2. It is very cold today.
   We are going to have very high temperatures this afternoon.
   Tomorrow it will be hot and sunny all day.
   It was windy on the coast yesterday.
   It is raining and there are lots of grey clouds in the sky.

68. Me and my mobile
1. Sample answers:
   1 Hay cuatro chicos.
   2 Todos tienen un móvil.
   3 Dos de los jóvenes escuchan música en el móvil.
   4 La chica a la izquierda muestra una foto a su amigo.
   5 Todos llevan pantalones.
2. 1 Los juegos son bastante divertidos.
   2 Cuidado, vas a romper la pantalla.
   3 Vamos a colgar unas fotos.
   4 Descargo vídeos y canciones.

69. Social media
1. (a) F (b) B (c) E (d) D
2. Read aloud text

Listen to the recording

70. The internet
1. (a) B (b) C (c) A
2. (a) She likes to make the holiday experience last.
   (b) She checks the weather (in the country she is going to) / She reads about the hotels before booking one.
   (c) She makes a list of places to visit.
   (d) a presentation with photos and comments
   (e) She likes to have a souvenir of the trip.

71. Computer games
1. Sample answer:
   T: ¿Qué vas a comprar?
   S: Quiero comprar un videojuego.
   T: ¿Para quién es?
   S: Es para mi hermana.
   T: ¿Qué tipo de juego quieres?
   S: Me gustaría un juego de acción.
   T: ¿Qué piensas tú de los videojuegos?
   S: No me gustan mucho.
   T: Vale.
   S: ¿Te gustan los videojuegos?
   T: Me gustan algunos.

Listen to the recording

2. (a) B (b) A (c) C (d) A

72. The good and the bad of technology
1. Sample answer:
En la primera foto hay un hombre con su portátil. El hombre tiene el pelo corto y marrón y lleva una camiseta gris. Creo que está en su casa, o en su oficina, no estoy seguro. Está mirando la pantalla de su portátil. Está muy enojado.
En la segunda foto una mujer está hablando con su hija y puede verla en la pantalla. Está muy contenta porque, aunque su hija vive lejos, todavía pueden estar en contacto gracias a la tecnología.

Sample answers to follow-on questions:
(a) Me parece muy útil. Nos permite hacer tantas cosas y podemos recibir mucha información. No sé qué haría sin Internet.
(b) Lo usé para ayudarme con mis estudios, para bajar música y para ver las noticias sobre mis grupos favoritos.
(c) Creo que dependemos demasiado de la tecnología y a veces, cuando no funciona, no sabemos qué hacer.
(d) Voy a usar los sitios web educativos para repasar antes de los exámenes. Tienen ejercicios muy útiles que ayudan a aprender las palabras que necesitas.

2 Sample answer:

Creo que la tecnología es increíble y muy útil. Es perfecta para mantenerte en contacto con la familia y los amigos, y tiene muchos usos diferentes. Uso Internet mucho para mirar los sitios web de mis artistas favoritos y ver vídeos de los cantantes que me gustan.

La semana pasada tuve un problema cuando estaba volviendo a casa y no pude llamar a mis padres en el móvil porque me quedé sin batería*.

Este fin de semana voy a subir unas fotos de mis vacaciones y mandaré mis deberes a mi profesor de historia por correo electrónico.

*me quedé sin batería = I ran out of battery

If you know language like this that is not on the AQA vocab list, you can still use it and be credited for it, as long as it is correct!

73. Places in town

1 (a) market – centre   (b) port – afternoon / evening
   (c) corner – friends
2 Sample answer:
   T: ¿Qué quieres hacer hoy?
   S: Me gustaría ir a la ciudad porque quiero ir de compras.
   T: ¿Qué quieres comprar?
   S: Quiero comprar una camiseta y un regalo para mi madre.
   T: ¿Algo más?
   S: Me gustaría ir al parque y ver la iglesia.
   T: Buena idea. ¿Cómo vamos?
   S: Podemos ir en autobús.
   T: Sí, de acuerdo.
   S: ¿Quieres comer en la ciudad?
   T: Me gustaría mucho.

74. Things to do

1 (a) A5 (b) E2 (c) B3 (d) F4
2 Irá de compras el martes.
   Visitará el castillo este fin de semana.
   Comeré / Cenaré en el café.
   Podrás jugar al fútbol el sábado.
   Veré una película en la plaza.

75. Shopping for clothes

1 (a) L (b) S (c) J (d) S (e) L (f) J
2 Sample answer:
   T: ¿Adónde vas de compras?
   S: Voy al centro comercial.
   T: ¿Con quién prefieres ir?
   S: Prefiero ir con mis amigos.
   T: ¿Qué piensas de comprar online?
   S: No me gusta.
   T: ¿Qué compras con tu dinero?
   S: Compro revistas de música.
   T: Yo también.
   S: ¿Qué tiendas te gustan?
   T: Me gustan las tiendas de moda.

76. Transport

1 To get to school previously / before I used to walk but now I go by bike.
   If I want to go to the city / to town, I usually catch the bus.
   It's not as comfortable as the train and it takes forty minutes. However, the tickets are cheaper.
   You can catch / get the boat to cross to the island.
2 Sample answer:
   En la primera foto vemos un tren con muchas personas. Las dos personas en el primer plano son una mujer y un hombre de negocios. Parece que los dos van al trabajo o a una reunión importante porque llevan trajes y camisas blancas. El hombre está hablando en su móvil. En la segunda foto, veo una calle de la ciudad con mucha gente. Algunas personas viajan en los autobuses, pero también hay muchos que van en bicicleta. Hay una mujer con una bolsa. Yo creo que va al trabajo. Hace mal tiempo.

Sample answers to follow-on questions:
(a) No está mal. Hay muchos autobuses que van con frecuencia a la ciudad. No tenemos una estación de trenes en mi pueblo, pero es fácil coger el autobús y luego coger el tren en la ciudad.
(b) Cogí el tren para ir a la ciudad y usé la bicicleta bastante.
(c) No me gusta nada. Es muy peligroso porque hay mucho tráfico.
(d) Voy a ir en autobús. Está demasiado lejos de mi casa para ir a pie.

77. Travelling on public transport

1 Sample answers:
   1 Hay un hombre.
   2 Lleva un traje gris.
   3 Está corriendo.
   4 El autobús está saliendo.
   5 Creo que el hombre va a perder el autobús.
2 (a) N (b) N (c) P (d) P+N

78. My region – the good and the bad

1 1 Hay edificios hermosos en esta ciudad.
   2 El paisaje en las montañas es tranquilo.
   3 Seguimos caminos estrechos por el bosque.
   4 Construyeron el polideportivo hace cuatro años.
   5 Permiten perros en esta zona.
2 Sample answer:

Vivo en esta región desde pequeña. Es una región bastante tranquila con mucho campo verde y pequeños pueblos. Por lo tanto, la gente piensa que es muy bonita y es popular entre los turistas. La ciudad donde vivo tiene varios edificios históricos y un gran parque al lado del río. Sin embargo, no hay mucho para los jóvenes y a veces parece un poco aburrida. Por eso, el fin de semana que viene, mis amigos y yo vamos a pasear en bicicleta por el campo y a hacer camping al lado del lago. Va a ser muy divertido. La semana pasada hubo una fiesta de comida en el parque y fui con mi madre para probar algunos productos típicos de la región. Pero también había puestos que vendían comida de otros países. Mi madre compró muchas cosas. Aunque todo era un poco caro, lo pasamos bien.

79. My region in the past

1 Read aloud text & sample answers to follow-on questions:
   (a) Aquí en mi pueblo no hay nada para los turistas, pero vivo cerca de dos ciudades importantes. Hay restaurantes buenos.
   (b) De momento estoy contenta aquí, porque toda mi familia y mis amigos están en esta ciudad, pero en el futuro me gustaría vivir en otro país un tiempo.
   (c) Doy paseos.
   (d) Estamos muy cerca de dos zonas muy bonitas. Hay muchos espacios verdes.
2 Hay muchos campos en mi región.
   No tenemos espacios verdes en la ciudad.
   Los vecinos en mi calle son muy simpáticos.
   Me gusta el parque al lado del río.
   Vivía en un pueblo pequeño.

80. Town or country?

1 (a) A (b) A+B (c) B (d) A (e) A (f) A+B
2 (a) B (b) C (c) B (d) B (e) A

81. The environment and me

1 Sample answer:
El transporte público en mi región no es muy bueno. No tenemos una estación de trenes y no hay muchos autobuses. Por eso, voy al instituto en bicicleta porque está bastante lejos de mi casa. Llego al instituto en unos veinte minutos.

La semana pasada, en el instituto, apagué todos los ordenadores al final de la clase de tecnología y ayudé a reciclar las botellas de plástico.

En el futuro, voy a ponerme más ropa y a bajar la temperatura en casa para usar menos energía.

2 Es muy importante proteger el planeta.
Debemos / Tenemos que hacer lo que podemos para cuidar el medio ambiente.
En nuestra casa, solemos reciclar el papel, las botellas y el plástico.
Cuando salí la semana pasada, usé el transporte público.
Mi hermana va a llevar su ropa a una tienda de segunda mano.

82. Local environmental issues

1 Sample answer:
La primera foto es de un grupo de ocho jóvenes trabajando en equipo para limpiar el parque en su barrio. Todos los miembros del equipo llevan una camiseta azul y están recogiendo la basura que la gente ha tirado. El parque parece estar en una ciudad. En la segunda foto varios niños y jóvenes están en un espacio verde, quizás en su instituto o en un parque. Llevan pantalones y camisetas. Hace buen tiempo y hace sol. Creo que están haciendo un trabajo muy importante para cuidar el medio ambiente y mantener los espacios verdes.

Sample answers to follow-on questions:
(a) Lo peor de mi pueblo es la cantidad de basura. La gente tira papel, botellas y bolsas de plástico en las calles y no les importa nada. Hay un grupo de personas que recoge la basura de vez en cuando, pero en mi opinión, no debería ser necesario.
(b) Cerca de mi casa hay un pequeño río y estaba lleno de basura. Yo pasé un fin de semana ayudando a limpiarlo para dar a los pájaros una zona más limpia donde vivir.
(c) Siempre apago las luces cuando salgo de una habitación y reciclo papel, vidrio y plástico.
(d) Debe construir otra carretera para quitar el tráfico del centro del pueblo.

2 Hay mucha contaminación en el mar.
Me gustan los espacios verdes en la ciudad.
Vamos a ir andando a la ciudad.
Mi madre odiaba el ruido de la carretera.
El aire está más limpio en el campo.

83. Global environmental issues

1 (a) A (b) C (c) A
2 1 Siguen talando muchos árboles en el bosque.
  2 Parte de la selva fue quemada.
  3 Los incendios son graves.
  4 En algunas zonas hay falta de agua.
  5 No saben cuándo vendrán las lluvias.

84. Caring for the planet

1 (a) C (b) B (c) A (d) C (e) A (f) B
2 Read aloud text & sample answers to follow-on questions:
(a) Lo primero es parar el cambio climático. Los gobiernos tienen que hacer mucho más. Tienen que bajar las temperaturas.

(b) Yo vivo en la costa y están intentando mantener las playas limpias. Esto es importante para la salud de los pájaros.
(c) En algunas zonas casi no llueve y hay una grave falta de agua.
(d) Ahorro energía.

85. A greener future

1 Sample answer:
En la primera foto puedo ver un grupo de niños con sus profesores. Están en el parque cerca de su escuela para estudiar la naturaleza. Están aprendiendo sobre las flores y los árboles. Tienen que responder a unas preguntas en un papel. En la segunda foto, un grupo de niños están en los jardines de su escuela. Están aprendiendo a cuidar los árboles.

Sample answers to follow-on questions:
(a) Me gusta dar paseos al lado de un río o del mar. Me gusta mucho estar cerca del agua y ver los peces y los pájaros.
(b) Sí, creo que es muy importante. Debemos aprender los efectos negativos que tenemos en el planeta.
(c) Tenemos un parque muy grande al lado del río que corre por la ciudad. También hay árboles en la calle principal.
(d) Creo que tenemos que parar el cambio climático porque es peligroso para el planeta.

2 El sol, el viento y el mar crean mucha energía.
Es energía limpia que causa menos contaminación.
Leí esta información en línea ayer.
Creo que el gobierno necesita gastar más en desarrollar / el desarrollo de estos recursos.
Será mucho mejor para el futuro del planeta.

86. Practice for Paper 1: Listening

1 (a) B (b) A
2 C, E, F
3 (a) E (b) D (c) B

87. Practice for Paper 1: Listening

1 (a) Maths, impossible (b) finishing, uniform
2 1 La actriz es una mujer inglesa.
  2 Sigo a esta estrella en los medios sociales.
  3 Su sueño fue tocar la guitarra.
  4 Va de gira en marzo.
  5 Cumple veinticuatro años el viernes próximo.

88. Practice for Paper 2: Speaking

1 Read aloud text & sample answers to follow-on questions:
(a) Mi ciudad es grande con muchas tiendas, restaurantes y oficinas. Hay un gran centro comercial y un cine moderno. El transporte es bueno.

(b) En mi opinión, es la contaminación del mar.
(c) Reciclo y no uso mucha energía en casa.
(d) Hay un parque en mi pueblo. También hay un bosque que es muy bonito.

2 Read aloud text & sample answers to follow-on questions:
(a) Soy una persona alegre y positiva y mis amigos me dicen que soy simpático. Me gusta mucho pasarlo bien y divertirme.

(b) Tus padres te dan toda su atención.
(c) Escucho música, veo la tele y hago mis deberes.
(d) Vamos al cine a veces.

89. Practice for Paper 2: Speaking
1 Sample answers:
   T: ¿Qué haces para estar en forma?
   S: Juego al baloncesto y hago natación.
   T: ¿Y qué comes?
   S: Como pescado.
   T: ¿Qué cosas prefieres no comer?
   S: Evito comer mucha sal y hamburguesas.
   T: Yo también.
   S: ¿Comes mucha comida vegetariana?
   T: Sí, todo el tiempo. ¿Qué vas a hacer este fin de semana?
   S: Voy a dar un paseo y leer una novela.

Listen to the recording

2 Sample answers:
La primera foto es de una playa en verano. Hay mucha gente tomando el sol y nadando en el mar. El cielo es azul sin nubes y la arena está muy limpia. Creo que hace mucho calor. A lo lejos veo edificios altos, probablemente hoteles y pisos. En la otra foto, una chica está de vacaciones en España y está visitando los sitios de interés. Lleva gafas de sol y una camisa roja. También tiene una mochila.

Listen to the recording

Sample answers to follow-on questions:
   T: ¿Qué piensas de las vacaciones en la playa?
   S: Me gustan mucho, si hay muchas actividades que hacer. Me gusta tomar el sol durante una hora, pero después es un poco aburrido. Me encantan los deportes acuáticos.
   T: ¿Te interesan las vacaciones culturales?
   S: Pues me gusta hacer visitas culturales durante mis vacaciones, pero también quiero pasar tiempo en la playa. Lo ideal es hacer las dos cosas.
   T: ¿Adónde van los turistas cuando vienen a tu país?
   S: Muchos van a la capital y a otras ciudades importantes e históricas. Otros buscan sitios más tranquilos como el campo o los típicos pueblos pequeños. No van a la playa porque no tenemos un buen clima.
   T: ¿Cómo se puede usar la tecnología para organizar las vacaciones?
   S: Es esencial hoy en día. Se puede buscar información sobre los sitios que quieres visitar, se puede escoger los restaurantes que te interesan y se puede reservar los vuelos, los hoteles y todo.
   T: Describe una actividad que hiciste durante las últimas vacaciones.
   S: El verano pasado pasé un fin de semana en un centro de actividades en el campo. Había un río y un gran bosque con muchos caminos para caminar o dar un paseo en bici. Había un montón de actividades para probar, como montar a caballo, nadar y jugar al tenis. Fue excelente y lo pasé muy bien.
   T: ¿Piensas que el turismo tiene un efecto negativo en un país?
   S: Es posible, sí. En algunos sitios, durante el verano, hay más turistas que habitantes. A veces dejan basura en las calles y hacen mucho ruido por la noche.
   T: ¿Qué sitio del mundo te gustaría más visitar?
   S: Me gustaría visitar España para participar en la Tomatina. Me parece una fiesta loca y muy divertida. Tengo la intención de ir algún día con un grupo de amigos.

90. Practice for Paper 3: Reading
1 (a) M (b) C (c) M (d) D (e) B
2 (a) A (b) C (c) B

91. Practice for Paper 3: Reading
1 (a) to look after (the) horses
  (b) help with horse riding classes
  (c) working in the shop / selling fruit (in the shop)
  (d) explaining the farm work to visitors
  (e) explaining the region's history
  (f) **A** (fruit)
2 We recycle glass and paper every week.
The flight leaves at half past eleven in the morning on Thursday.
I am very happy because I passed the IT / ICT exam.
The number of accidents will go up if we do not solve the problem.
The pupil was punished for breaking the rules several times.

92. Practice for Paper 4: Writing
1 Sample answers:
  1 Hay un chico.
  2 Está en el salón.
  3 Está haciendo sus deberes.
  4 Tiene un ordenador.
  5 Hay una guitarra.
2 Sample answer:
Voy a las tiendas los sábados. Prefiero ir a la ciudad o al centro comercial porque las tiendas son mejores allí. Voy con mis amigos normalmente, pero a veces voy con mi madre. Las tiendas en la ciudad son buenas y hay mucha variedad. Me gusta comprar ropa y revistas.
3 (a) nuestra (b) salir (c) hago (d) está (e) del

93. Practice for Paper 4: Writing
1 Para tener una vida sana, es importante hacer ejercicio.
Voy a levantarme temprano mañana.
Cuando estaba de vacaciones, vi una película al aire libre.
El ordenador / El portátil está roto y no puedo hacer mis deberes.
Un cantante español / Una cantante española ganó el concurso europeo el año pasado.
2 Sample answer:
Me gusta mucho estudiar idiomas y creo que son muy útiles en el mundo. La gente piensa que todo el mundo habla inglés, pero no es verdad. Me encanta hablar español cuando voy a España porque sorprende a la gente.
Para los últimos exámenes, estudié mucho. Usé actividades en línea y leí mis libros. Hice exámenes del pasado y aprendí palabras nuevas. También estudié con mis amigos.
En el futuro, me gustaría trabajar en una empresa con oficinas en otros países. Me encantaría viajar con mi trabajo o trabajar en el extranjero. (92 words)

94. Nouns and articles
1 (a) la (b) el (c) las (d) los (e) la (f) el (g) las (h) los (i) el (j) la
2 (a) las (b) un (c) el (d) los (e) una (f) un (g) el (h) El
3 (b) Mi padre es ~~un~~ policía y mi madre es ~~una~~ médica.
  (c) Hay muy pocos estudiantes en el instituto sin ~~un~~ móvil.
  (d) Escribo con ~~un~~ bolígrafo en mi clase de matemáticas.
  (e) En el futuro me gustaría ser ~~una~~ actriz.
  (h) Se puede reservar dos habitaciones con ~~una~~ ducha.

95. Adjectives
1 (a) cómoda (b) contentos (c) rojo (d) interesantes (e) español (f) simpáticas (g) bonita (h) baratos
2 (a) moderno (b) cómodos (c) bueno (d) emocionante (e) limpia (f) útiles
3 (a) En Inglaterra hay **poca** gente que habla muy bien alemán.
  (b) Lo mejor es que tiene un jardín **bonito**.
  (c) Estamos **contentas** porque hace buen tiempo.
  (d) En el futuro habrá una **gran** estación en las afueras de la ciudad.
  (e) Mi abuela vive en el **primer** piso.

96. Possessives and pronouns

1

English	Spanish singular	Spanish plural
my	**mi**	**mis**
your	**tu**	tus
his / her / its	**su**	**sus**
our	**nuestro / nuestra**	nuestros / nuestras
your	**vuestro / vuestra**	**vuestros / vuestras**
their	su	sus

2 (a) Mi (b) Su (c) Sus (d) Mis (e) Su
3 (a) el mío (b) las suyas (c) el nuestro (d) el tuyo
4 (a) María tiene un gato que es negro y pequeño.
  (b) Vivimos en un pueblo que está en el norte del país.
  (c) En la clase de inglés tengo que leer un libro que es muy aburrido.

97. Comparisons

1 (a) Mi madre es **más alta que** mi padre.
  (b) Marta es **menos seria que** Francisco.
  (c) Este autobús es **más lento que** el tren.
  (d) La fruta es **tan sana / saludable como** las verduras.
  (e) Esta camisa es **tan cara como** aquel vestido.
2 (a) el mejor (b) los peores (c) la más pequeña
  (d) las más difíciles (e) las menos aburridas
3 (a) Mi primo / a es más fuerte que tu tío.
  (b) Su móvil es pequeñísimo.
  (c) El examen de español es facilísimo.
  (d) Las películas de aventura son tan emocionantes como las películas de acción.
  (e) ¡Mi instituto es el más viejo / antiguo!
  (f) Las ciencias son menos aburridas que la geografía.
  (g) Mi amigo Martín es nuestro mejor jugador.

98. Other adjectives

1

Masc. sing.	Fem. sing.	Masc. plural	Fem. plural
este	**esta**	**estos**	estas
ese	esa	**esos**	esas
aquel	**aquella**	aquellos	aquellas

2 (a) estas camisetas (b) esta camiseta (c) aquella chica
  (d) esos huevos (e) ese móvil (f) aquellas revistas
  (g) este libro (h) esa película (i) aquel tren (j) estos platos
  (k) esas naranjas (l) aquellos chicos
3 (a) cada (b) misma (c) algunos (d) todos (e) otra
4 (a) Todos (b) Algunos (c) Todos (d) algunos (e) misma
  (f) mismas

99. Pronouns

1

yo	I
tú	you singular
él	he
ella	**she**
nosotros	we (masc.)
nosotras	**we (fem.)**
vosotros	**you plural (masc.)**
vosotras	you plural (fem.)
ellos	**they (masc.)**
ellas	they (fem.)

2 (a) Las hemos perdido.
  (b) La han perdido.
  (c) Teresa lo come.
  (d) Lo compro.
  (e) No la bebo.
  (f) No la lavo.
  (g) Lo quiero escribir. / Quiero escribirlo.
  (h) No quiero leerla. / No la quiero leer.
3 (a) I am going to write to him / her this afternoon.
  (b) I visited them yesterday.
  (c) I will do it if I have time.
  (d) I gave him / her a present for his / her birthday.
  (e) Have you seen them?
  (f) Vino a visitarme en casa. / Me vino a visitar en casa.
  (g) Me mandaron la información.
  (h) Voy a comprarlos en línea. / Los voy a comprar en línea.

100. The present tense

1 (a) vivimos (b) bailan (c) vendo (d) lleváis (e) odias
  (f) come (g) salimos (h) escucha
2 (a) comen (b) vivimos (c) tienes (d) hablan (e) debe
  (f) grita (g) hablo (h) lee (i) piensa (j) Podéis
3 (a) cenamos (b) trabajan (c) tomo (d) pone
  (e) compramos (f) cuestan (g) Quiero (h) piden

101. Reflexive verbs

1

me	levanto
te	levantas
se	levanta
nos	levantamos
os	levantáis
se	levantan

me	siento
te	sientes
se	siente
nos	sentimos
os	sentís
se	sienten

2 (a) se (b) se (c) Te (d) se (e) se (f) Nos (g) os (h) Te
3 Todos los días Olivia **se levanta** temprano para ir a trabajar. **Trabaja** en una tienda de ropa famosa. Primero **se lava** y **se viste**. **Baja** la escalera y **toma** el desayuno. Siempre **se sienta** en la cocina para comer. Después **se lava** la cara en el cuarto de baño que está abajo, al lado de la cocina. **Se pone** los zapatos y **sale** a las ocho y media porque el autobús llega a las nueve menos cuarto. **Vuelve** a casa a las siete de la tarde.

102. Irregular verbs (present)

1 (a) tengo, tienes (b) da, doy (c) oye, sale (d) hace, cojo
  (e) venís, traéis
2 (a) oye (b) conozco (c) vienen (d) cojo (e) vamos (f) sé
  (g) tienes (h) pongo (i) traigo (j) dicen
3 (a) Voy a España. (b) Tiene dos hermanas. (c) Oigo música.
  (d) Dice la verdad. (e) Cogemos el autobús.
  (f) Hacen los deberes. (g) Sales los sábados. (h) Doy clases.
  (i) traigo (j) dicen

103. *Ser* and *estar*

1 (a) está (b) son (c) Soy (d) es (e) Son (f) está (g) Estáis
  (h) Estamos
2 (a) Where is the bank? (*estar* for location)
  (b) My grandmothers are very nice. (*ser* for characteristics)
  (c) I am from Madrid but I work in Barcelona. (*ser* for where you are from)
  (d) The dress is green with white flowers. (*ser* for colours)
  (e) It's four thirty in the afternoon. (*ser* for time)
  (f) The bed is next to the door. (*estar* for location)
  (g) You are (all) very sad today because the holidays have finished. (*estar* for moods)
  (h) We are ready for the history exam. (*estar* for meaning 'ready' not 'clever')
3 (a), (d), (e)
  (b) Mi amigo es alto y tiene el pelo negro.
  (c) Me duele la cabeza y estoy enfermo.
  (f) Mi madre es médica y mi padre es ingeniero.

104. The gerund / present participle

1 (a) comiendo – eating
  (b) estudiando – studying
  (c) corriendo – running

(d) tomando – taking (drinking / eating)
   (e) diciendo – saying / telling
   (f) recibiendo – receiving
   (g) escribiendo – writing
   (h) escuchando – listening
   (i) aprendiendo – learning
   (j) viendo – seeing
2 (a) Estoy escuchando música.
   (b) Están navegando por Internet.
   (c) Estamos viendo una película.
   (d) Estás hablando con amigos.
3 (a) Estaban comiendo cuando su madre les llamó.
   (b) Estábamos tomando el sol cuando empezó a llover.
   (c) Estabas cantando cuando salió el tren.
   (d) Estaba jugando a los videojuegos cuando llamó.
   (e) Estábais escuchando al profesor cuando entró la directora.
   (f) Estaba estudiando en la biblioteca cuando oyó el ruido.

105. The preterite tense
1 (a) sacaron (b) volvimos (c) compró (d) llegaste
   (e) trabajasteis (f) fue (g) di (h) tuvimos (i) pidieron
   (j) leyó
2 (a) fui (b) tuvimos (c) dieron (d) fue (e) dio, pagué
   (f) fueron (g) dijo (h) fue (i) Hice (j) tuve
3 **Fui** al cine con mis amigos y **vimos** una película de acción. Después **comimos** en un restaurante. **Comí** una hamburguesa con ensalada, y mi amiga Lola **comió** pollo con patatas fritas. **Bebimos** agua y mi amigo Juan **tomó** una naranja pero yo **tomé** un café. Después del restaurante **fui** en tren a casa de mi prima. El viaje **fue** largo y aburrido. **Volví** a casa y **me acosté** a las once de la noche.

106. The imperfect tense
1 (b) De pequeños nadábamos en el mar todas las semanas. ✓
   (c) Había mucha gente en el museo y los cuadros eran muy bonitos. ✓
   (e) Cuando eran más jóvenes, no comían fruta ni verduras. ✓
   (h) Estaba nervioso cada vez que hacía una prueba de matemáticas. ✓
   (j) Nevaba todos los días y hacía un frío horrible. ✓
2 (a) On Wednesday we went to the swimming pool and we swam for an hour and a half. (preterite for completed action in the past)
   (b) When we were little, we used to swim in the sea every week. (imperfect for 'used to')
   (c) There were a lot of people in the museum and the pictures were really lovely. (imperfect for descriptions)
   (d) My father prepared a vegetarian meal for us. (preterite for a completed action in the past)
   (e) When they were younger, they didn't eat either fruit or vegetables. (imperfect to describe repeated actions in the past)
   (f) Gabriela arrived in Madrid by train to start her new job. (preterite for completed action in the past)
   (g) Yesterday we met in the café and we talked all afternoon. (preterite for completed action in the past)
   (h) I used to be nervous every time I did a maths test. (imperfect for 'used to')
   (i) I had a very good time because it was sunny and it didn't rain. (preterite for completed action in the past)
   (j) It snowed every day and it was horribly cold. (imperfect for descriptions)
3 (a) tenía (b) vivía (c) estaba (d) lavé (e) trabajaban
   (f) gastó (g) comíamos (h) jugué

107. The future tense
1 (a) jugar (b) Va (c) a (d) voy (e) Vas (f) Vais (g) va
   (h) ir (i) vamos (j) Voy

2 (a) Vamos a ver la película.
   (b) No trabajaré los lunes.
   (c) Van a coger el metro.
   (d) Irá a Sudamérica.
   (e) Van a jugar con mi hermano.
   (f) Irás a España.
3 (a) va a ir (b) voy a ir (c) voy a pasar (d) voy a vivir
   (e) voy a viajar (f) vamos a visitar (g) vamos a probar
   (h) Va a ser

108. The conditional tense
1 (a) compraríamos – we would buy
   (b) saldrían – they would go out
   (c) trabajaríais – you (all) would work
   (d) estaría – he / she / it would be
   (e) jugarías – you would play
   (f) vendríamos – we would come
   (g) podrías – you could
   (h) habría – there would be
2 (a) iría (b) tomarían (c) trabajaría (d) ganaríamos
   (e) habría (f) usaría (g) tendría (h) lucharían
   (i) ganaría (j) compartiríamos
3 NB All answers can use either *podrías* or *deberías*. Some answers are interchangeable.
   (a) Podrías leer para descansar.
   (b) Podrías comer más frutas y verduras.
   (c) Deberías hacer más ejercicio.
   (d) Deberías ir al médico.
   (e) Deberías acostarte temprano.
   (f) Podrías ir al dentista.
   (g) Deberías usar menos energía.
   (h) Podrías comprar ropa de segunda mano.

109. The perfect tense
1

	haber (in present tense)	+ past participles
	(I have …, etc.)	(spoken, eaten, lived, etc.)
yo	he	
tú	has	hablado
él / ella / usted	ha	comido
nosotros / nosotras	hemos	vivido
vosotros / vosotras	habéis	
ellos / ellas / ustedes	han	

2

Infinitive	Irregular past participle	Scrambled version
hacer	hecho	beatiro (abierto)
volver	vuelto	cheoh (hecho)
abrir	abierto	cidoh (dicho)
romper	roto	lutove (vuelto)
ver	visto	sotupe (puesto)
escribir	escrito	tisvo (visto)
poner	puesto	toro (roto)
decir	dicho	triseco (escrito)

3 (a) We have lost our car.
   (b) Have you studied Spanish?
   (c) They have bought a computer.
   (d) I have done my homework.
   (e) We have seen a very informative programme.
   (f) Me he roto el brazo.
   (g) Han perdido la maleta.
   (h) Hemos comido muchos caramelos.
   (i) ¿Has visitado el museo hoy?
   (j) Los profesores han abierto las ventanas.

110. Giving instructions
1 (a) Sube a la derecha. (b) Cruza la plaza. (c) Pasa el puente.
   (d) Ten cuidado. (e) Ven aquí. (f) Canta más bajo.
   (g) Lee en voz alta. (h) Escucha bien. (i) Bebe agua.
   (j) Haz este ejercicio.
2 (a) Subid a la derecha. (b) Cruzad la plaza.
   (c) Pasad el puente. (d) Tened cuidado. (e) Venid aquí.
   (f) Cantad más bajo. (g) Leed en voz alta.
   (h) Escuchad bien. (i) Bebed agua. (j) Haced este ejercicio.

3
tú commands	*vosotros / as* commands
(a) Baja la música.	(a) Comprad las verduras en el mercado.
(b) Haz la cama.	(b) Escoged vuestros cuartos / vuestras habitaciones.
(c) Visita el museo.	
(d) Canta con la música.	(c) Discutid el problema primero.
(e) Sal antes de las seis.	(d) Reciclad esas botellas.
	(e) Corred en el parque, no en la calle.
(f) Siempre di la verdad.	(f) Limpiad / Lavad el coche el domingo.

111. The present subjunctive
1 (a) haga (b) tengas (c) venga (d) sea (e) vayas (f) tenga
   (g) sea (h) vaya (i) haga (j) vengas
2 (a) vayas (b) hagas (c) seas (d) venga (e) haga (f) tengas
3 (a) Mi hermana quiere que haga la cena.
   (b) Me molesta que no vengas conmigo.
   (c) Espero que tengas suerte con los exámenes.
   (d) Cuando vayas a España, debes visitar Barcelona.
   (e) Puedes ir a Sudamérica cuando seas mayor.

112. Negatives
1 (a) No estudio geografía.
   (b) No vamos a la ciudad.
   (c) Ricardo no compró una bicicleta nueva.
   (d) Sus padres no vieron la tele.
   (e) No voy a ir a España la semana próxima.
2 1 H 2 E 3 A 4 B 5 G 6 C 7 D 8 F
3 (a) No como nada durante el descanso.
   (b) En mi familia nunca tuvimos un perro.
   (c) Aquí no tengo ni vestidos, ni faldas, ni camisetas.
   (d) No vas a comprar ningún coche.
   (e) Mis padres no escuchan a nadie.
4 (a) Por la tarde nunca bebemos / tomamos café.
   (b) No canto, ni bailo, ni toco (ningún) instrumento musical.
   (c) No hablan ningún idioma.
   (d) No podemos hablar con nadie durante el examen.
   (e) Nunca fumaré porque es malo para la salud.

113. Special verbs
1
me		I like
te		you like
le	gusta (sing)	he / she / it likes
nos	gustan (plural)	we like
os		you (all) like
les		they like

2 (a) A Paula le gusta …
   (b) ¿Te gustan …
   (c) Nos interesa …
   (d) A Manuel le duele …
   (e) Le encanta …
   (f) No me importa …
   (g) ¿Te duelen …
   (h) No me interesan …

3 (a) Acabo de ver una película muy buena / buenísima.
   (b) Lleva dos horas trabajando en el jardín.
   (c) Nadia acaba de terminar su carrera universitaria / en la universidad.
   (d) Llevamos un mes viviendo aquí.
   (e) Tus abuelos acaban de salir.

114. *Por* and *para*
1 (a) For my birthday I want a new mobile phone.
   (b) My friend works for an international company.
   (c) Apps for the iPhone are incredible.
   (d) I eat a lot of vegetables and fish in order to keep fit.
   (e) You need rice to make a paella.
   (f) Smoking is very bad for your health.
2 (a) El coche rojo pasó por las calles antiguas.
   (b) Normalmente por la mañana me gusta tomar huevos con pan.
   (c) Mandé la información por correo electrónico.
   (d) Me gustaría cambiar este vestido por otro.
3 (a) Para (b) para (c) por (d) por / para (e) para

115. Asking questions
1 Why? – ¿Por qué?   Where to? – ¿Adónde?
   What? – ¿Qué?   Which? – ¿Cuál?
   When? – ¿Cuándo?   Which ones? – ¿Cuáles?
   How? – ¿Cómo?   How much? – ¿Cuánto?
   Where? – ¿Dónde?   How many? – ¿Cuántos?
2 (a) Dónde (b) Cuándo (c) Cuáles (d) Cuánto
   (e) Qué (f) Cómo (g) Adónde (h) Cuántas
3 (a) Where does Mario live?
   (b) When are you going to arrive, boys?
   (c) Which of these glasses are mine?
   (d) How much money am I going to need for the holidays?
   (e) What do you think of the new teacher?
   (f) How are we going to travel? On the underground or by / on the bus?
   (g) Where are you going to take your friends (to) when they come?
   (h) How many people were in the stadium for the match?
4 1D, 2G, 3A, 4H, 5B, 6C, 7E, 8F

116. The passive
1 (a) fue escrita (b) serán construidos (c) es usado
   (d) son limpiadas (e) fueron presentados
   (f) fue reconocida
2 (a) The novel was written last century.
   (b) The flats will be built next year.
   (c) The sports centre is used by thousands of people every week.
   (d) The facilities are cleaned every day.
   (e) This morning the students were presented / introduced to the head teacher / director.
   (f) Last night the actress was recognised several times in the restaurant.
3 (a) Se publicarán (b) Se mandarán (c) se basa
   (d) Se organiza (e) Se limpió (f) Se robaron

117. Numbers
1 (a) veinte 20 (b) cuarenta y ocho 48
   (c) nueve 9 (d) cien 100 (e) catorce 14
   (f) mil 1 000 (g) trescientos 300 (h) cincuenta y siete 57
   (i) veintitrés 23 (j) quince 15 (k) diecinueve 19
   (l) quinientos 500 (m) un millón 1 000 000
   (n) novecientos 900 (o) ochenta y ocho 88
   (p) setenta y seis 76 (q) sesenta y siete 67 (r) diez 10
   (s) cero 0 (t) veintinueve 29

2 (a) mil novecientos noventa y nueve
(b) el diez de octubre
(c) el primero / uno de enero
(d) el tres de marzo
(e) dos mil trece
(f) el dieciséis de noviembre
(g) el treinta de mayo
(h) mil novecientos sesenta y ocho
(i) dos mil dos
(j) el veintiuno de abril

3 (a) Son las siete y cuarto.
(b) Es la una y veinticinco.
(c) Son las nueve menos veinticinco.
(d) Son las once y diez.
(e) Son las cuatro menos cuarto.
(f) Son las diez menos diez.
(g) Son las cinco y media.
(h) Son las doce.

118. Paper 1: Listening (Foundation)

1.1	B	5.2	science fiction	8	Meal 2 When P
1.2	A	5.3	special effects	9	Meal 3 When F
1.3	C	5.4	very expensive	10.1	D
2	B C D	6.1	C	10.2	F
3.1	B	6.2	A	10.3	A
3.2	C	6.3	C	11	N
3.3	C	7.1	B	12	P
4	D C F	7.2	C	13	N
5.1	favourite director	7.3	A		

Dictation
Sentence 1: No salgo cuando llueve.
Sentence 2: Vivo en una zona tranquila.
Sentence 3: La ciudad es hermosa pero ruidosa.
Sentence 4: La gente era muy amable.

121. Paper 2: Speaking (Foundation)

Role play
Sample answer:
T: ¿Cuál es tu asignatura favorita?
S: Mi asignatura favorita es el inglés.
T: ¿Qué piensas de tu uniforme?
S: Es muy feo.
T: ¿Qué haces durante el recreo en el instituto?
S: Hablo con mis amigos.
T: ¿Cuándo haces tus deberes?
S: Hago mis deberes después de la cena.
T: Ah yo también.
S: ¿Te gustan tus profesores?
T: Me gustan mis profesores.

Reading aloud and sample answers to follow-on questions:
(a) Mando mensajes, llamo a mis amigos y uso internet.
(b) Me gusta ver vídeos divertidos.
(c) Me gustan porque son interesantes, pero a veces son peligrosas.
(d) Tengo ordenadores en las clases de informática y a veces hago ejercicios en línea.

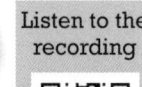

Photo card
Sample answer:
En la primera foto, hay un chico en el salón de su casa. Está solo y está jugando a un videojuego en su ordenador. Lleva pantalones y una camisa azul. En la otra foto

hay un grupo de cinco chicos y están jugando al fútbol en un jardín o un parque. Están contentos.
Sample answers to follow-on questions:
T: ¿Qué te gusta hacer en tu tiempo libre?
S: Me gusta pasar tiempo con mis amigos, escuchar música y jugar al fútbol.
T: ¿Qué actividades haces con tus amigos?
S: Vamos al cine, jugamos a los videojuegos y a veces hacemos camping.
T: ¿Cómo celebras tu cumpleaños normalmente?
S: Salgo a cenar en un restaurante con mi familia y a veces vamos a un parque temático.
T: ¿Qué tipo de música prefieres?
S: Mi música favorita es la música rock.
T: ¿Cuándo escuchas música?
S: Escucho música en mi dormitorio y en el autobús cuando voy al instituto.
T: ¿Qué tipo de programas ves en la tele?
S: Veo programas divertidos y de deportes.
T: ¿Cuáles famosos sigues en las redes sociales?
S: No sigo a personas famosas, como actores, pero sigo a mis bandas favoritas.
T: Háblame de una persona famosa que te gusta.
S: Me gusta el cantante inglés Tom Grennan porque tiene una buena voz y sus canciones tienen letras interesantes.
T: ¿Qué deportes te interesan?
S: Me encanta el fútbol y a veces voy con mi padre al estadio para ver a nuestro equipo.
T: Háblame de un concierto al que fuiste.
S: Fui a ver Green Day el año pasado. La música fue genial y compré una camiseta.

122. Paper 3: Reading (Foundation)

1	B		20	P+N
2	A		21	N
3	C		22	P
4	C		23	P
5	A		24	C
6	B		25	B
7	A D F		26	A
8	B		27	C
9	A		28	B
10	A		29	A
11	A		30	B
12	It was very slow. / It was difficult / hard to understand.		31	A
			32	C
13	a love story / romantic film		33	learn to swim / have swimming lessons
14	people eating / people talking		34	not much parking space
15	He can stop / pause the film (when he wants).		35	It has a view of the pool. He can see / watch his children in the pool.
16	A		36	increase water temperature
17	B			
18	B		37	B
19	A+B		38	B

Translation
39 I want a job / I want work **(1)** during the summer holidays. **(1)** I would like to learn **(1)** to play a musical instrument. **(1)** We had a party **(1)** after the exams. **(1)** (reject festival) My cousin is spending **(1)** a year abroad. **(1)** (reject passing) I am going to upload **(1)** these photos from my mobile. **(1)** (reject go up)

128. Paper 4: Writing (Foundation)
Sample answers
1. Hay una mujer famosa.
   Lleva un vestido largo y gris.
   Muchos jóvenes hacen fotos.
   Hay un hombre con traje negro.
   El hombre lleva gafas.
2. Como pollo, ensalada y pan. A veces como pescado.
   No como caramelos y prefiero no tomar mucha sal.
   Me gusta salir a correr y voy a la piscina los viernes.
   En mi tiempo libre escucho música y veo películas.
   Voy al cine con mis amigos o al centro comercial. (49 words)
3. 3.1 gustan
   3.2 comprar
   3.3 para
   3.4 me
   3.5 Cuántas
4. No llevo gafas.
   Trabajo en un café los sábados.
   Vamos a estudiar en la biblioteca.
   Mi perro duerme en la cocina.
   Había mucha basura en las calles.

5.1
En mi región muchas veces voy al parque con mis amigos para jugar al baloncesto. También los fines de semana damos un paseo en bicicleta en el campo. En verano nadamos en el río.
El fin de semana pasado, ayudé mi grupo local a limpiar la basura de las calles. Mucha gente tira papeles y botellas de plástico y es muy feo.
La casa de mis sueños estaría en la costa, al lado de la playa, con un gran jardín. Tendría una piscina y un gimnasio y muchos dormitorios para todos mis amigos. (93 words)

5.2
Me gusta bastante mi instituto. Es grande y tiene muchos edificios modernos, pero también tiene algunos edificios viejos. Los profesores son simpáticos y nos ayudan mucho con nuestros estudios.
El año pasado el instituto organizó un viaje a York. Fui con mis compañeros de la clase de historia. Fuimos a un museo muy interesante y aprendimos mucho. El viaje en autobús fue un poco aburrido, pero escuché música.
El año que viene, creo que voy a estudiar matemáticas, informática y ciencias. Pienso que voy a ir a la universidad después, pero no estoy seguro. (94 words)

129. Paper 1: Listening (Higher)

1	N	8.2	very expensive	14	She is saving for her holidays.
2	P	9.1	B		
3	N	9.2	A	15	B
4	Food 2	9.3	B	16.1	E
	When A			16.2	D
5	Food 3	10.1	C	16.3	B
	When C	10.2	B		
6.1	A	10.3	C	17	Topic D
6.2	C	11.1	B		Information from 4
6.3	B	11.2	A		
6.4	C	11.3	A+B	18	Topic A
7.1	favourite director	12.1	hottest		Information from 2
		12.2	rain	19.1	A
7.2	science fiction	13	to pay his phone bill	19.2	C
8.1	special effects			20.1	B
				20.2	C

Dictation
Sentence 1: Participaron en el desfile de la Nochebuena.
Sentence 2: Se hizo daño en el pie.
Sentence 3: Estaba lloviendo cuando salí del colegio.
Sentence 4: No entiende algunos conceptos de química.
Sentence 5: La presentadora tiene muchos seguidores.

133. Paper 2: Speaking (Higher)
Role play
Sample answer:
T: ¿Qué es lo bueno de tu región?
S: Me gusta la gente, y mis amigos viven cerca.
T: ¿Qué aspectos no te gustan?
S: La calle mayor es un poco fea y hay algunas tiendas vacías.
T: ¿Cómo es el clima?
S: Llueve todo el tiempo.
T: ¿Adónde fuiste el fin de semana pasado?
S: Fui al parque y jugué con amigos.
T: ¡Qué bien!
S: ¿Cómo es tu ciudad?
T: Es muy moderna. Me gusta mucho.

Reading aloud & sample answer
to follow-on questions:
T: ¿Qué haces para descansar?
S: Voy a mi dormitorio para escuchar música o para ver una película en mi portátil.
T: ¿Por qué es importante tener actividades que hacer en tu tiempo libre?
S: Es importante no estudiar todo el tiempo. Las actividades físicas son buenas para el cuerpo.
T: ¿Cuáles son las ventajas de ser famoso?
S: Normalmente los famosos tienen mucho dinero y sin duda es una ventaja ser rico. Puedes comprar lo que quieres.
T: ¿Cuál es la mejor manera de celebrar tu cumpleaños?
S: Lo mejor es ir a un parque temático.

Photo card
Sample answer:
En la primera foto una chica está dando un regalo a su abuela. El regalo está en una caja. Creo que es su cumpleaños. Están en la casa de la abuela y hay unas flores allí también. Creo que la chica quiere mucho a su abuela. En la segunda foto, un chico y su hermana están en la cocina y toman el desayuno. El chico tiene el pelo corto y marrón, y una camiseta azul y gris. La chica tiene el pelo largo y una camiseta gris. Los dos llevan gafas. Están discutiendo y el chico está enojado con su hermana. Pienso que se pelean mucho.
Sample answer to follow-on questions:
T: Describe la personalidad de un amigo tuyo.
S: Mi amigo, Tom, es un chico muy divertido y animado. Me hace reír mucho y es muy buena compañía. Es muy deportista y le encantan los animales.
T: ¿Cómo es esta persona físicamente?
S: Es muy alto, el más alto de la clase, y tiene el pelo corto y rubio y los ojos azules. Las chicas piensan que es muy guapo.
T: ¿Cómo debería ser un amigo o una amiga ideal?
S: El amigo ideal debería ser comprensivo y debería compartir los mismos intereses que tú. Tiene que ayudarte si tienes un problema y estar ahí cuando lo necesitas.
T: ¿Qué hiciste con tus amigos la semana pasada?
S: Fuimos al centro comercial y compré un regalo para mi hermana porque es su cumpleaños en una semana.
T: ¿Crees que tienes una vida sana?
S: Sí. Bastante. Tengo una dieta equilibrada, pero a veces como una hamburguesa y patatas fritas. Hago mucho ejercicio, pero no voy al gimnasio cada día como algunas personas.

T: ¿Qué tipo de comida prefieres evitar?
S: No me interesan los postres y por eso no suelo comer muchas cosas con azúcar. Nunca como caramelos.
T: ¿Qué deporte haces en el instituto?
S: Se puede escoger entre varios deportes durante el año. Yo suelo escoger el fútbol y el baloncesto.
T: ¿Qué tipo de actividades te gusta hacer en clase?
S: Me gusta hacer actividades con un compañero o con un grupo. Prefiero resolver problemas, o discutir temas.
T: ¿Como es la comida en tu instituto?
S: No está mal. Ofrece cosas que no son muy sanas, pero siempre puedes encontrar algo como una ensalada, o pollo con arroz, y siempre tienen fruta.
T: ¿Cuáles son tus planes para tus estudios en el futuro?
S: Creo que voy a continuar mis estudios en el instituto, o hay la posibilidad de ir a otro instituto. Voy a escoger tres asignaturas para hacer. Creo que estudiaré inglés, historia y español, pero depende de mis notas en los exámenes.
T: ¿Qué tipo de trabajo buscarás en el futuro?
S: Voy a hacer más investigación durante los próximos años porque no tengo idea del tipo de trabajo que quiero.

134. Paper 3: Reading (Higher)

1	P+N	23	A+B
2	N	24	B
3	P	25	You get a discount of 2 euros. / You pay 2 euros less to enter.
4	P		
5	C	26	hot and cold meals / dishes
6	B	27	climb trees
7	A	28	A
8	C	29	C
9	C	30	B
10	A	31	the sons and daughters of very rich people
11	B		
12	A	32	She is the daughter of one of the cleaners.
13	C		
14	Satisfied with E Not satisfied with C	33	that he didn't get the job
		34	what he can do to improve for the future
15	Satisfied with F Not satisfied with D	35	He would have got on with the others (in the team).
16	A, B, C		
17	P	36	He did not know much about the company / firm. **OR** He did not know much about the work they did / their work.
18	F		
19	P		
20	N		
21	A+B		
22	B		

Translation

My brother is very clever / smart **(1)** and (he) looks a lot like my father / is just like Dad. **(1)** (reject ready and seems like) (The) Mexicans are proud of their festivals / fiestas **(1)** like The Day of the Dead. **(1)** I have just been for a walk / stroll **(1)** at the side of / by / along the river. **(1)** The bullring is no longer / The bullring isn't **(1)** used for bullfights / bullfighting any more. **(1)** I prefer to watch (the) matches / to see the games **(1)** live in the stadium. **(1)**

140. Paper 4: Writing (Higher)

Sample answers

1
Generalmente / Normalmente nos llevamos muy bien con nuestros abuelos.
A veces me levanto tarde los fines de semana.
Voy a leer todas las opciones antes de escoger mis asignaturas.
No quiso / quería salir ayer porque hizo / hacía frío.
Lo bueno de mi región es el clima.

2 (a)
En mi región muchas veces voy al parque con mis amigos para jugar al baloncesto. También los fines de semana damos un paseo en bicicleta en el campo. En verano nadamos en el río.
El fin de semana pasado, ayudé a mi grupo local a limpiar la basura de las calles. Mucha gente tira papeles y botellas de plástico y es muy feo.
La casa de mis sueños estaría en la costa, al lado de la playa, con un gran jardín. Tendría una piscina y un gimnasio y muchos dormitorios para todos mis amigos. (93 words)

2 (b)
Me gusta bastante mi instituto. Es grande y tiene unos edificios modernos, pero también tiene algunos edificios viejos. Los profesores son simpáticos y nos ayudan mucho con nuestros estudios.
El año pasado el instituto organizó un viaje a York. Fui con mis compañeros de la clase de historia. Fuimos a un museo muy interesante y aprendimos mucho. El viaje en autobús fue un poco aburrido, pero escuché música.
El año que viene, creo que voy a estudiar matemáticas, informática y ciencias. Pienso que voy a ir a la universidad después, pero no estoy seguro. (94 words)

3 (a)
En mi pueblo no tenemos muchas fiestas, pero en verano hay una semana cuando hay un festival. Hay una exposición de pinturas en la biblioteca y hay conciertos en los institutos y en la iglesia. También hay juegos para los niños en el parque. Creo que las fiestas en España son mucho más interesantes y emocionantes. Algunas son famosas en todo el mundo, como Las Fallas o La Tomatina. Un día, me gustaría participar en la Tomatina. Sería muy divertido.
Hace dos meses mi madre celebró su cumpleaños y mi hermana y yo decidimos preparar una cena especial. Compramos todas las cosas del supermercado y pasamos todo el día en la cocina preparando la comida. Hicimos dos platos calientes y para después una ensalada de frutas porque a mi madre no le gustan mucho los platos dulces. No era de la calidad de una cena en un restaurante, pero mi madre estaba muy feliz. (154 words)

3 (b)
Lo peor de las redes sociales son los comentarios horribles que algunas personas escriben. Son mensajes de odio y no son necesarios. Pueden tener un efecto muy malo en chicos jóvenes, y a veces las víctimas son niños bastante pequeños. También, algunos jóvenes pasan horas mirando estas redes y están perdiendo su tiempo cuando podrían estar haciendo algo más activo o educativo.
Hace unos meses mi hermano mayor dejó su tarjeta de crédito en una tienda. No sabía qué tienda era porque estaba en una ciudad donde estaba trabajando ese día. Sin embargo, miró un plano en Internet y encontró la tienda. La información en Internet le dio el número de teléfono de la tienda y usó su móvil para llamar. Le guardaron la tarjeta hasta el día después cuando fue a buscarla. Yo creo que con la tecnología puedes resolver fácilmente problemas que antes eran imposibles. (149 words)